#myvoice

#myvoice

A Collective Memoir by Women of Substance From Around The World

GLOBAL INFLUENCERS PUBLISHING HOUSE
152 Prince Charles Cr, #17-12 Singapore 159013
Website: www.globalinfluencers.sg
Email: contactus@globalinfluencers.sg
First Published in Singapore by
Global Influencers Publishing House 2021

Title: #myvoice
ISBN: 978-981-18-1310-8

GLOBAL INFLUENCERS PUBLISHING HOUSE

Printed and bound by Redflame Publishers

Contents

Gratitude

We would like to extend our heartfelt gratitude to Mrs. Purviz R. Shroff MH and the late Mr. Rusy M. Shroff BBS. MBE., for supporting the publication of the book and helping us, raise the voices of these brave and courageous women so they are heard.

Preface

Our voices are one of our most valuable possessions. It is an essential tool for communicating with the world around us. It can be both vocal and written. Both can be quiet, and both can be a roar!

To have a voice is to have some measure of power. According to the United Nations, the empowerment and autonomy of women and the improvement of their political, social, economic, and health status is a significant end in itself. In addition, women's voices are crucial to creating inclusive, open, and prosperous societies.

However, it is a well-known fact that women's empowerment doesn't come without challenges. Often women find themselves caught in a convoluted web and at the short end of the stick. The pathways of women's progress are riddled with biases, discrimination, and other obstacles.

In this book, 23 women from across the world raise their voices to share their inspiring and heart-warming stories. These women are the unsung heroes and community champions who have gone above and beyond their course of work, service and passions, providing extraordinary examples of courage, resilience, triumph, kindness, compassion, self-love, transformation, skill and success.

Some of the stories told are deeply personal. How does it feel to know that you cannot bear children when this is a basic human desire? What is it like to fall terminally ill when you are living a healthy life? How do you find your voice when you feel so small and powerless that you literally cannot speak? What do you do when life seems to hold no hope for the future?

Every chapter in this volume, no matter the content, is about finding one's authentic voice. They are lessons in perseverance, honouring your life purpose and recognising that age is no barrier to achieving your soul purpose and ultimately happiness. By learning to understand yourself, you too can reach that point and place where one can say, "That's what I was always meant to do."

Examples set by these women will serve as inspiration, encouragement and proof that anything is possible when you take action. It celebrates exceptional accomplishments and achievements, a shift from living ordinary lives to being extraordinary achievers.

Singapore Children's Society

Founded in 1952, the mission of Singapore Children's Society is to bring relief and happiness to children in need. The Society protects and nurtures children and youth of all races and religions. In 2020, the Society reached out to 34,654 children, youth and families in need.

Singapore Children's Society currently operates 12 service centres, offering services in the four categories of: Vulnerable Children and Youth, Children and Youth Services, Family Services, and Research and Advocacy.

Funds raised through the sale of this volume will support the work of the Society which includes being a voice for our children and their future.

We are grateful for the trust that the authors and publishers of this book have shown in supporting our work. Without their collective voices this book would not exist.

For further information and to support the Society, visit our website at *https://www.childrensociety.org.sg/*

STORY ONE

All For the Love of Pumpkins

To Live is to Give. Service to Humanity is Service to God.

For someone who doesn't know me, to hear me say "I love my Pumpkins" will be unexpected.

I am clearly neither a gardener nor a farmer, but I have cultivated the lives of many children, and these are the Pumpkins with a capital "P" to whom I refer.

You see, all my life from a very young age, I have loved children.

Although I have now spent most of my life in Hong Kong, I am originally from India.

Born in Calcutta, I grew up and went to school in Pune. I have very fond memories of living in Pune with my immediate family and many relatives surrounding us.

One of the most impactful influences in my life was my mother, Mrs. Hilla Moogat. Not only did she raise seven children with my father, but she was also the first lady School Principal in Bulsar, Gujarat.

It is my parents who taught me the life values that I hold firm to this day. The gifts of gratitude and empathy being two of the key values to which I aspire.

Constantly being surrounded by children at a young age, I decided to study child psychology and then specialise in teaching children. I even taught in Mumbai at the Queen Mary school for a few years.

Since then, I have always been with babies and children – touching, hugging, teaching, guiding, and nurturing them.

One of the most critical changes in my life occurred when I got married to Rusy in 1970. I had to conform quickly to my new lifestyle. Following my heart, I ran a small kindergarten in Hong Kong. Simultaneously, I maintained an active social life.

People assume that when one is blessed with good fortune (by working hard, I might add), everything is always easy and perfect. Sadly, this is not so.

My husband had overcome many challenges in his life. Including being imprisoned by the Japanese during the Second World War. While this experience alone could embitter someone for the rest of their lives, for my Rusy, it served to strengthen his desire and need to be a charitable man. In his lifetime, he contributed to many charities in Hong Kong.

In spending time with my husband, I developed my charitable gifts. I continue to serve and support many NGOs and charitable foundations in Hong Kong and overseas. Naturally, when you serve the community for an extended period, there comes recognition of your work.

It humbles me to be the recipient of such awards, the most recent being the Medal of Honour (M.H.) by the HKSAR Government for outstanding and dedicated community and charitable service. Particularly my contribution to Hong Kong Tuberculosis, Chest and Heart Diseases Association and Mother's Choice – awarded in 2018. None of them is ever expected, and they are most certainly not why I choose to support organizations or do the work I do.

My work is mostly focused on children, mothers, and the underserved. This is where I can be of most service. Having worked with children for so long, I can empathise when they are in need. I know that a loving hug or a non-judgmental ear is, at times, more valuable than any amount of money. I am always filled with gratitude that I have the capacity to offer this and more to those who truly need assistance and support.

Giving to others is also, some may think surprisingly, the greatest gift I can give to myself. To watch others blossom and fair well is what makes my heart sing. It is often the smallest hand up, not hand out, making the biggest difference in a young person's life. A smile or a hug given to me holds more value to me than any amount of money or any award.

But life has not always been a bed of roses, and I, too, have had my fair share of devastation and sorrows.

One Father's Day, the phone rang. I expected that it would be our son, Zarir, calling for his father. Instead, it was my distraught daughter-in-law calling to let us know that our beloved son had been killed unexpectedly in a road accident in Switzerland.

No one can imagine what losing a child means. As parents, it is our job to show our children a path to follow. To lose one's child before their full potential is met is a devastation of the highest order and a challenge of the greatest kind to one's personal resilience. It is a breaking point for many parents!

But in my case, something opposite and miraculous happened. After Zarir's death, I had a vision of him telling me to be brave and to carry on doing what I loved – singing to children. Soon after this vision, I was introduced to Mother's Choice.

Mother's Choice is an independent, community-based, non-profit organization offering support to small children, teenagers, and women in need of care, counseling, or shelter due to unintentional pregnancy or other domestic conflicts.

I was a volunteer there for over 25 years, eventually becoming Patron. I would go and be amongst the babies, my Pumpkins, four days a week. I would sing them the lullabies that I had sung to my son. This is what my son had wished for me in the vision I had of him after his death. This organization, above all others, brings the most joy to my heart. It is here that I spend most of my time touching, hugging, and singing lullabies to the babies - my beloved Pumpkins.

One of the greatest joys in my life is when one of my Pumpkins writes a personal note to thank me. I have personally cared for more than 2,600 babies, and every one of them is dear to me. To see them improve in their health and to learn of their successes are my gifts to myself.

Sometime after our son Zarir's death, we endowed the Ruttonjee Hospital with the Zarir Rusy Shroff Ward. By doing this, we were able to create a legacy for our son and transform our personal tragedy into an act of kindness for the Hong Kong community.

What a gift it was for both Rusy and I to be able to do this. One of the greatest combined achievements of both of us. A lasting legacy long after I am gone.

In 2017, when my dear Rusy passed away, I was distraught but told myself that life must go on. More importantly, I must carry on the good work we started together. My heart has overflowed with joy to see the difference my humble work has made to so many mothers and children.

I have been fortunate to have some amazing souls who have inspired me throughout my life. Starting with my late mother Hilla, highly respected Mr. and Mrs. JH Ruttonjee, my dear Rusy, and all those who have taught me the value of perseverance, dedication, and forgiveness.

But, here I must say that you don't have to have wealth or lots of time to contribute to something that makes your heart sing. If you find that small way to contribute to the wellbeing of humanity, you should pursue it in whatever small way you can. The gifts that come back to you in return will far exceed any small sacrifice you may have to make.

With the hindsight of someone who has lived a long, happy, and rewarding life and to quote my late husband: "To Live is to Give. Service to Humanity is Service to God."

About The Author

Mrs. Purviz R. Shroff, MH is well known for her numerous contributions to children and their welfare.

She is Patron of Mother's Choice, and President of the Hong Kong Tuberculosis, Chest and Heart Diseases Association.

Together with her husband the Late Rusy M. Shroff, BBS, MBE, she has supported many local charitable organizations such as Women Helping Women Hong Kong, Hong Kong Cancer Fund, The Hong Kong Anti-Cancer Society, Riding for the Disabled Association, Hong Kong Society for the Protection of Children, Lifeline Express Hong Kong Foundation, Youth Diabetes Action, Save the Children Hong Kong, and many more. They have also set up scholarships and bursaries at various institutions.

Mrs. Purviz R. Shroff, MH also served as the Permanent Managing Director of Ruttonjee Estates Continuation Limited for many years.

Mrs. Purviz R. Shroff, MH can be contacted at:

Website: *https://www.motherschoice.org/en/*

STORY TWO

And Then Came the Biggest Curveball

When we face up to the challenges that life throws our way, we discover what we are really made of.

I didn't expect it to happen to me. A 52-year-old mum of two young children, I had deliberately set myself up for success. I was a health freak. I exercised at least five times a week, ate a low-carb diet, rarely touched sugar (oh, but how I enjoyed a good glass of wine or three!), and I never smoked. I intended to live to 100.

It was August 2020, and I was tired. I assumed menopause was wearing me down. I ached a little, but perhaps I was overdoing it at the gym. And I had an annoying sore throat that was making it difficult to sing. I didn't want a silly ulcer to slow me down.

Only it wasn't an ulcer. It was advanced stage IV Non-Small Cell Lung Cancer. The mild discomfort I had felt was, in fact, three large tumours: two in my lungs and one covering my thyroid. The disease was aggressive and had already spread to multiple parts of my body – my liver, bones, adrenal glands, and more. The likelihood of living to see my next birthday was slim.

The diagnosis shattered me. It wasn't death that concerned me. It was the unbearable thought of leaving my beautiful children, Saffron and Austin, without a doting mother and my beloved husband, David, without his life partner. And, with the pandemic keeping us apart, the idea that I might never see my parents and sisters again shook me to the core.

But in time, my thoughts gave way to something stronger. As I took stock of my life and all that I've done to get to where I am today, a steely resolve to live life on my own terms took over. I had a choice: how I reacted and responded to cancer was up to me. I could not allow this disease to define or defeat me. I decided to do everything I possibly could to beat cancer one day at a time.

While cancer is by far the greatest lesson and – as I now see it – the greatest gift I've ever had, I reflected and realised it was the lessons along the way that might help me move forward.

I've always believed I am a lucky person. I still do. But, to a large extent, we generate our own luck, and serendipity is a part of the mindset of many successful people.

I was born into a vibrant Scottish family where love was in abundance, but money was tight. The first to go to university, I worked split shifts in a restaurant to pay my own way through a degree in Psychology followed by a Masters in IT. I started as a waitress, trained as a chef, and finally became duty manager. It was tough and tiring and, outside of work and studies, I didn't have a social life. But, in that time, I learned to be independent, an effective team member, and manage people and money.

After graduating, I was determined to find a job that would lay my money worries to rest. I moved to London and started my investment banking career at JP Morgan. To say I was thrown in at the deep end supporting traders first in London and then on Wall Street is an understatement, but I loved my work and the opportunities to learn. Soon, I was leading global IT programmes, moving into Chief Operating Officer roles and covering Europe, Middle East, and Africa, and then Asia. I finally had all that I'd worked so hard for: the alpha female banker lifestyle with a warehouse apartment, sports car, and lots of opportunities to travel.

I was 37 years old when I met David. Together, we moved to Singapore, had our first daughter, and then moved to Hong Kong. Sustaining my career became increasingly difficult. I was struggling to get the right balance. We wanted another child, but I was working such long hours, I barely saw David and couldn't spend time with my baby girl.

I decided to leave my banking career and take the lessons I'd learned to carve out a new career: one that would make the best use of my experiences, allow me to pursue my passion for people development, and give me the space to embrace motherhood.

After training extensively, I became an accredited executive coach and set up my own Diversity & Inclusion consultancy. Working with global financial services firms, I now help people become successful at work and support women and underrepresented groups to break through barriers. And, after a lot of effort and modern medicine, I had my sweet little son at the age of 45. Life was good. I had a purpose-fuelled career, I spent time with my family, and I had the space to do the things I love like choral singing and trail running.

Then came cancer. Only days before, I had spoken during a radio interview about how our best careers and lives are ahead of us. I took some time to reflect on what I had shared and determined how best to apply them in my situation. It occurred to me that I could harness all my life learnings to help heal my body and manage my mind. I have the resources within.

The first task at hand was to break the news to my loved ones. Thankfully, my oncologist encouraged me not to use the "C" word for a while when speaking with my children. The news was incredibly difficult for David, particularly as he is an only child who had lost both his parents to cancer when he was quite young. The conversation with my parents and sisters in the UK was perhaps the most challenging I have ever had.

The next task was to implement a holistic strategy, which in part meant understanding the cause of lung cancer – a silent killer which claims more lives than any other cancer. I was surprised to learn that globally, half of all lung cancer patients are women who, like me, were healthy and had never smoked. In Asia that figure rises to 60-80%. A growing number of female non-smoker cancer patients are in their 30s and 40s. Outwardly healthy and blissfully unaware of the disease raging within, most people discover they have lung cancer only when it has spread and is terminal.

It wasn't smoking that caused my cancer. It was stress! Like many women who are carrying the load during the pandemic, I was juggling home learning support with work deadlines. On top of that, I was trying to complete a house purchase in the UK. And then there was the rollercoaster ride of menopause to cope with too. I was physically, mentally, and emotionally exhausted and my immunity had taken a hit.

My first glimmer of hope came when my oncologist advised that I have a genetic mutation that responds to targeted therapy. Instead of chemotherapy, I could take one pill a day to kill off the cancer cells for one or two years. It would return, he said, but he was hopeful there might be a new, more effective treatment. If not, I would have to undergo chemotherapy.

Determined to take ownership of my health and wellbeing, I reached out to supportive friends, so they could share any leads that might help me. I was introduced to a clinical researcher in Australia who had scoured the world to find the best practitioners and treatments to support her husband with stage IV colon cancer. She alone saved me months of time.

As David read through all the research papers and medical claims, I connected with recommended integrative oncologists, naturopaths and dieticians across the globe who, because of the pandemic, could be consulted virtually. Together, we devised a strategy that included supplements, "repurposed drugs," and an immunity-boosting diet – all known to stall cancer growth.

To protect my bones, which have small holes in them where the cancer has been, I committed to daily weight training exercises, monthly injections, and supplements. To restore inner calm and positive energy, I engaged in twice-weekly acupuncture and energy healing sessions, infrared saunas, breathing exercises, yoga, and meditation.

After two weeks of targeted therapy, my oncologist advised that my cancer blood markers had gone from extremely high to normal. He was amazed – he had never witnessed such a quick response. Over the next few months, I continued to respond well to the treatment and added intensive radiotherapy to the biggest tumours in my lung and liver.

In April 2021, I received the news I'd so desperately longed for complete remission from my cancer. I was thrilled! There is currently no evidence of the disease in my body. I'm hopeful that the strategy I have in place will allow me to stay in remission for a long time. If it doesn't, I intend to face the next stage of my life journey with positivity and perseverance.

I know how lucky I am to have made it this far. Despite courageously battling cancer, millions of lives are lost to the disease every year. I'm also aware of how blessed I am to be living in Hong Kong, where we have access to amazing medical treatment and private healthcare.

A firm believer in the mind-body connection, cancer has made me question my values and revisit my life purpose. I've taken my experience as a message to step back and evaluate how I choose to show up in the world. I'm determined to emerge from this experience a better person. I have a new purpose – to heal myself and return better and brighter than ever before and to share my learnings in the hope that it might help others cope with life challenges too.

As a leadership coach, I offer science-backed tips to help clients empower themselves at work. Some of those tips have empowered me in life, both before and during cancer. Today, I'm sharing them with you:

1. **Get a great support team in place**. Be it at work or in life, it is important to surround yourself with strong and supportive people that can step up for you in different circumstances.
2. **Take ownership** – I often tell clients to take ownership of their careers and lives and don't let others do it for them. Empower yourself, advocate for yourself, make informed decisions. It's your life. Own it.
3. **Master your mind**. Wash out negative, toxic emotions. Instead, activate your parasympathetic system, which is responsible for stimulation

of "rest-and-digest." In this way, we can heal. To activate it, we need to be calm and rested. Meditation, deep breathing, gratitude – these are all powerful, science-backed ways to help you cope with life's challenges.

4. **Define and follow your purpose.** Your purpose is not what you do; it is who you are. Understanding your purpose in life and applying that to your work can massively enhance your results and give you a newfound sense of satisfaction. Not only that, research indicates purpose can increase longevity… and I am living proof of that!
5. **Focus on doing what you love.** When I got sick, many people expected me to give up work and stop doing the things I enjoyed. Instead, I have streamlined my life. I don't work full-time; I've stopped overscheduling, and I continue to follow my passions like singing which, in addition to bringing me joy, is proven to improve my lung capacity. I now spend more quality time with my children, family, and friends, and really value our time together.
6. **Never give up hope.** This is one of the most important tools we have. Believe that things will get better. We cannot predict the future so why waste time imagining the worst. And when we face

up to the challenges that life throws our way, we discover what we are really made of.

As Harriet Beecher Stowe said: "Never give up, for that is just the place and time that the tide will turn."

About The Author

Shirley Adrain is a Diversity and Inclusion Consultant, Leadership Coach and Corporate Trainer for global banks and professional services organisations across Asia.

She began her two-decade career in Wall Street and has since worked in London, Singapore and now Hong Kong. In 2017 Shirley founded and became CEO of Career Catalyst Group (CCG).

Her financial leadership roles include COO and global Chief of Staff for Tier 1 investment banks like JP Morgan and Citigroup. Shirley has a monthly programme on RTHK Radio 3 and regularly speaks on D&I focussed event panels.

A keen classical singer, she has performed in Carnegie Hall and the Lincoln Centre. Despite always being health conscious, Shirley was diagnosed with terminal lung cancer in 2020.

Overcoming the initial shock of her real limitations (ageing, disease and death) Shirley drew on her professional learnings to help her move past her imagined limitations (time and resources) and now lives from her deeper, more authentic self.

Shirley can be contacted at:

Email: *shirley@careercatalystgroup.com*

LinkedIn: *https://www.linkedin.com/in/shirleyadrain/*

Website: *https://www.careercatalystgroup.com*

STORY THREE

Become Your Own Heroine

It's a scorching tale that awakens you to the full suite of your heroine's majestic soul-fire gifts, power and talents; alchemising all painful experiences into fuel for even greater self love, faith, wisdom and ultimately victory.

Introduction: The Invocation

The journey of Becoming Your Own Heroine is about leaning into those soul-defining, soul-shaping moments that change you forever, with the aim of no longer hanging back or hiding out in fear. This is where we must learn to pay attention from the heart, as this is where our soul is being called to transform.

Picture your heart being lit with a giant alchemical match, the purpose of which is to ignite your soul-fire awakening. Let the initiations begin! Pray, breathe and take heart as you enter this arena called life. Hold your head up high with complete blind faith that your character is about to be reshaped into a soul-fire diamond that is ready and able to withstand anything. For this, I can surely promise, you're ready, and you're prepared to go into this ring we call life, as I now share with you my poignant, heartfelt story.

Section 1: Life Before Loss

Have you ever woken up feeling like there is a giant internal tug of war inside you? You experience night terrors as you struggle to begin another day, yet something within you is pulling you to awaken from the slumber of the life you've been living. "Wake up!" it's crying out to you. "Wake up, will you, please?"

Several years ago, I got to a point in my life when I was waking up and reliving who I was over and over again, and hating every minute of it. It broke me.

In the deepest recesses of my soul, I knew until I brutally came face to face with my own truth I did not stand any chance of living the life my soul was born to live, to break out of the mold, to break out of convention, to break with society and most importantly, to heal my individual and collective shadow selves.

To break free from our ordinary, expected, conventional and smaller selves is to afford the soul freedom to live an extraordinary and magical existence, sourced from within the greatest realized part of ourselves.

The question that naturally arose for me was: "How do I do this? How do I access this greater part of myself, to live the life my soul intended and become the person I was born to be?"

The answer I received was in no way what I expected, nor was it something that I consciously desired to receive. And yet, it was clear, this is how my soul is choosing to answer it right now. I'm to listen, hold space, pay attention, and most importantly: get the hell out of my own way!

Section 2: Devastating Loss

I will never forget the evening of 4 July, 2019. It is a date that is forever etched in my memory because it was the day that a part of me died, with the unexpected and tragic news of my husband's sudden passing. I emerged from the wreckage of this news, traumatised, destroyed, my heart and soul broken in two. I had no words, only tears, and no part of me could even stay in my body long enough to process it, as it was too big and overwhelming for my internal system to comprehend. My world had been rocked to the core.

My husband was my pillar and my rock, and it felt like my safety and security blanket had been taken away from me. I felt so far away from anything and anyone who felt familiar and who felt like home to me. At that moment, I felt like God, the Universe, the Divine, and Life had picked up their collective bags and just walked out on me. And it was in that devastating moment, I felt like my life ceased to have any real meaning or value. I saw no point in being here.

In this place of existential crisis, I began a process of deep soul searching. Internally, externally – you name it – I was looking for God or meaning everywhere. The seeker in me just could not rest or settle; there was an incessant hunger to understand. I could not make sense of where I found myself. I did not just want to find answers. I was demanding that God give them to me.

Now, there was this giant question mark looming over me: "Why am I here? What's my purpose for being here?" I remember the desperate pleading with God to tell me why my husband had been taken, for what purpose, and why now? I was so angry. I felt betrayed. Before I even had time to blink, I had gone from wife to widow, the hope and promise of our new life together withered and dead.

I remember staring up at my bedroom wall, begging God for answers. God was silent, and it was only over a gradual period that my soul started whispering to me the answers I was seeking: life is a mystery, life is not forever, life cannot be taken for granted. It is fleeting, fragile and precious, and we must live it with our whole, complete heart.

"Great," I thought, now I'm being told that my life is impermanent. I breathed and waited for my soul to answer. It said: "Answers will come slowly; live within the questions. Sometimes the truth that must be accepted may be very painful to the human form, but your soul knows what I am speaking of. The love between your husband and you is eternal, and that love will remain with you forever."

At that moment, my human self could not grasp this. I missed my husband's physical presence. I was now having to come to terms with the idea that I was going to have to live my life on my own and that, on a soul level, our contracts on this earth had in fact been completed. God had taken him for a bigger purpose, and here I was on earth coming to terms with all that remained.

Section 3: Going Into the Fire

When I was coming to terms with my husband's death and my broken, shattered life without him, the place where I went to find salvation and to hold me was Mother Nature. I didn't know it at the time, but Mother Nature was holding me in her divine womb when I felt empty, lonely, destroyed, and covered in heart scars from the pain of my losses. It was she that was guiding me and whispering to me at my lowest points.

I remember the soul-fire awakening moment as if it was yesterday. I was in my parents' garden, and there was a fire burning. I saw everything had turned to ashes, a lot like what had happened to me with my husband. I said to myself: "Our soul returns to where it belongs, and yet it rises from the ashes."

And I thought to myself: "All this pain, all this suffering, all this trauma. What if I can burn it in the fire and become one with the fire, rise like the fire and through this process transmute my pain into some kind of new beginning?" Mother Nature had been grooming me to see that I was in an alchemical cycle, one of death and rebirth, one of descending and rising, one of going from holding on to letting go.

And in the flickering moments between pain and alchemy, I got glimpses into the truth that my pain could serve a higher purpose. In the resurrection from my pain, I could rebirth myself from pain to power, or pain to wisdom, and that it was part of my soul-fire awakening in this lifetime to learn what there is to learn from letting go and merging with my fire of true becoming.

This is when my fear turned to excitement, and instead of focusing on what I was losing, I could now, for the first time, see what I was gaining through harvesting, composting and re-forming myself in my fire. I began to see that this would be my access point to share with others, to have people transmute their pain, their struggle, and their losses into something truly alchemical and magical.

I've learned it's not possible to live an awakened life without walking straight into the wreckage and pain of your old life and without confronting it head-on. When you embrace your shadows and integrate them into your life, then you're truly doing the work of living an Awakened Spiritual Life.

Section 4: The Heroine's Journey

When you go through the process of deconstruction to reconstruction, and you emerge from your own true soul-fire awakening, there is an all-important soul shift that needs to take place for you to go from a place of surviving in your life to one of winning and mastering your life. And fundamentally, that means throwing onto the fire the victim mentality, the perspective we've all grown up with, and shifting to choose to live your life from a place of authenticity, living from your unadulterated truth. What I have come to call – living from an 'unbullshitifed' life.

Section 5: Embodying the Warrior Goddess Spirit

It is during life's greatest trials and tribulations that the Warrior Goddess is truly shaped and formed. She moves through a massive process of unlearning who and what she has been taught to be. She begins to let go of past, unconscious layers of external belonging and comes to the realization that the only person she truly belongs to is herself.

From then on, she listens only to her wise inner compass, her heart, to guide her out the other side of the challenges, the attacks, and the losses. The Warrior Goddess spirit is formed in the dark, in the shadows, and through the pain. By becoming one with her pain and suffering, she comes to an all-important epiphany: the only way she will get through the trials and tribulations is by consciously choosing to be on her own side and to stay there.

At this point, she powerfully chooses herself, and by merging her shadows with her light, she arrives at a welcoming place of peace within. She becomes totally at one with her flaws. She becomes "flawsome!"

Section 6: Building Unbreakability

From this incredibly dangerous place of freedom, you now operate on an entirely game-changing frequency or dimension. Now nothing anyone says or does will rock or shake you the way it did in the past.

You have learned what it truly is to become "unmessable" and "unbreakable" within yourself. When you cross that threshold, it becomes permanently encoded within you, and there is this thrilling feeling of "I've gone too far now. There is no turning back!" You've fundamentally altered your internal set point, and this is when the whole game of your life changes. It is in this hot, incessant, pressurised state that you're being formed and shaped into a diamond!

Through the combination of excruciating pressure, a barrage of attacks, and at times what felt like insurmountable challenges, I discovered it was my indomitable will and indestructible strength that, time after time, carried me across my own victorious finish line. I recognised that my pain was forming into an unshakeable inner strength and source of resources and power, which I was able to summon within myself, much like a super heroine turning it on at any time, at will, and whenever I needed it. Instead of being afraid, I can now willingly embrace, surrender to and welcome it, because I realise that no one was going to break me. And that's when the entire tide of my life changed.

Finale: Becoming Your Own Heroine

To sum up, until you've walked the Heroine's Journey, you have not yet walked the journey of truly coming home to yourself. Until then, our heart door remains open, unfulfilled, waiting for our soul to answer the most deep-seated and pressing call we'll ever have, which is the call to be ourselves.

About The Author

Pari*Pascale Seiler is Co-Founder, pioneering Change Agent and Visionary Artist behind the Awakening Light School, a modern day Harry Potter School for adult souls to awaken and rise into their greatest expanded selves. She is also the Founder and Director of Intuity World, Asia's first business committed to bringing inner wisdom and awakening change for real-world success and business solutions.

She is here to precipitate the largest feminine collective movement of awakening ever known by teaching us all how to radiate from our divine feminine presence, in service of realizing a new earth.

Born and raised in Hong Kong, Pari*Pascale blends the passion of the West with the loving wisdom of the East. She is a renowned Awakening Light Coach, Soul Transformational Healer, Feminine-Centered Self Actualizing Facilitator, Radio Host and co-author of the book Ready Aim Captivate, featuring alongside Deepak Chopra.

Pari*Pascale can be contacted at:

Website: *http://www.simplynaturaltherapies.com.au/practitioners/pascale-seiler/*

LinkedIn: *https://www.linkedin.com/in/pascale-seiler/*

Facebook: *https://www.facebook.com/intuityworld*

STORY FOUR

Facing Your Deepest Fears

My big bully was anxiety, an inner voice telling me to do things that made no sense and that my world would fall apart if I didn't meet its demands.

Imagine a child playing with her friends on a bright sunny day when all of a sudden, a bully appears, causing the child to freeze and her friends to scurry. The bully crowds her, screams at her, calls her names, breaks her toys, and demands her lunch money, even threatening to punch her in the face if she doesn't comply. In the face of this booming voice and big personality, this innocent child feels helpless and hopeless.

This child was me when my anxiety disorder was at its worst in my late twenties. My big bully was anxiety, an inner voice yelling at me to do things that made no sense and telling me that my world would fall apart if I didn't meet its demands.

But I didn't let the bully win. I didn't buy into its lies. I fought for myself. I challenged and stood up to the bully and overcame a debilitating anxiety disorder. I won.

Going through this battle of the mind gave me a high level of empathy and compassion for sufferers of mental illness. This motivated me to start my own mental health charity in 2018. To raise awareness of mental health in a part of the world where it is still largely a taboo topic became my life's purpose.

In 2008, I went from being a happy-go-lucky primary school teacher who loved to be around people, to a woman wracked with fear, worry, and anxiety in the blink of an eye. My greatest fear was death, and I couldn't run from it. Death is the one certainty of life. Everyone will die, with no exceptions! This statement in itself paralysed me to the core.

Since the age of four, I was scared of death like most children are, but instead of talking about my fears, my parents comforted me and did what they thought was best to prevent me from feeling fear.

When I turned 28, I was faced with a series of traumatic events – the death of three close family members in six months, and I did not have the skills or support that I needed to cope. All I remember was long periods of mourning, having to wear white, funerals, and thinking about how fine the line was between life and death.

These events reminded me of my mortality, and my anxiety spiralled out of control. Suddenly, I developed an irrational belief that if I was in contact with anything related to death and dying, it would cause me to die.

The fear of death was so intense that I wasn't able to write the word "death" on a piece of paper, couldn't pass a mortuary or even hug someone who had lost a loved one without it causing tremendous anxiety. Intellectually, I knew that my thought was irrational and logically nothing would happen to me if I did any of these things but emotionally, I didn't believe it.

My world became scary and unsafe, and I craved reassurance and control. I would constantly ask questions of those around me to make sure that I wouldn't die after being exposed to a death-related phenomenon. This caused my family and close friends a lot of frustration as they couldn't understand why I was behaving in this way. My anxiety disorder was so severe that it impacted my ability to conduct daily tasks, work, and relationships.

Having studied Psychology as an undergraduate student, I quickly realised what was happening to me. I developed Obsessive Compulsive Disorder (OCD). OCD is a severe anxiety disorder that is made up of obsessions and compulsions. Obsessions are unwanted, intrusive, and disturbing thoughts that repeatedly play in one's mind like a song that is stuck in one's head.

Obsessions cause a high level of distress and anxiety to sufferers that lead to the performance of compulsions, repetitive behaviours to temporarily relieve anxiety, and prevent perceived negative outcomes from occurring.

My OCD was severe, and I needed help. It took real courage to speak to my family about my fears as there is so much stigma, misconception, and judgment associated with mental illness, especially in Asia. Being told to think positive, to pray more, to not overthink things, or that I was acting crazy were just a few of many comments I had to deal with. Although this was hurtful, I knew I needed professional therapy to reframe my thinking and face my irrational fears.

With the unconditional support of my sister and my best friend, I received intensive treatment in cognitive behavior therapy (CBT) and Exposure Response Prevention (ERP), scientifically proven methods in treating anxiety disorders like OCD.

The road to recovery was a tough one and required immense commitment and determination to get better. I wouldn't wish OCD upon anyone. Therapy was beyond challenging.

I learnt skills to be able to live a normal life with a great set of tools to manage my anxiety. I learnt that I could be around "death," and nothing would happen to me. The ultimate goal of therapy was to cope with intrusive thoughts and anxiety without allowing them to control me and stop the compulsions that compounded the disorder.

CBT work involved questioning my irrational beliefs. This process of questioning allowed me to realise that the irrational thoughts I had were not real and just fear-based. It wasn't my fault that I needed help seeing this as that is what an anxiety disorder does. It clouds your vision and alters the brain's chemicals and biology responsible for happiness, safety, and logic.

ERP is a critical part of treatment for OCD. With ERP, sufferers of anxiety disorders and OCD are exposed to feared stimuli in a gradual and manageable way.

Facing your deepest fears requires a lot of emotional strength, and this was the time for those muscles to develop. I had to face "death" in different ways every day, be it going to a cemetery, sleeping with the word death written all over my body, or going to a funeral on Diwali day.

I remember the first time I had to go into a cemetery, the thought of walking into an open space filled with tombstones petrified me. We had to start slowly, the first step was to just sit in a car next to the cemetery with the windows cracked open, to ultimately walking around a cemetery in the middle of the country on my own for two whole hours which felt like a lifetime.

After enduring these exposures to death, my anxiety level was extremely high, and I was told that the only thing I was allowed to do was feel my anxiety. I could not call a friend, shower off anything I felt was negative, wash my hands, change my clothes or think about something happy to feel better. All I was allowed to do was to feel the feelings of anxiety, breathe, and wait for the anxiety to reduce and pass. At the time, this seemed impossible, like complete torture and many questions filled my mind. How could I just sit there and feel my fear?

I spent every day of the week for five months intensively working on myself at therapy and for two years after that as I no longer wanted OCD to be part of my life.

My day at therapy was structured to include: three hours of identifying and challenging fear-based thoughts, six hours of facing my fears, and the remaining two hours of the day doing art therapy or relaxation activities. I made great friendships that I treasure with other sufferers in therapy and have nothing but gratitude for my therapist, who really encouraged me to face my fears, gave me tough love, and never stopped believing in me, even when I doubted myself.

After experiencing CBT and ERP, I learnt that anxiety is a big liar eagerly waiting to stop you from living your life and to rob you of any joy that you feel. I learnt that the only way to eliminate anxiety is to experience it, and although it feels awful, it is not dangerous, and it won't kill you. Anxiety does pass, it doesn't stay forever, and if you allow yourself to feel the emotion and do what scares you the most repeatedly, it will go down over time; this is known as habituation.

My experience and journey with an anxiety disorder inspired me on both a professional and personal level. It encouraged me to become a cognitive behavior therapist specialising in the treatment of OCD and anxiety disorders to help others who are struggling.

When I work with clients, I understand them from a personal experience as well as from the knowledge that I acquired during my training. My clients feel like I really get them because I have been there before and made it through to the other side.

While I was studying to become a therapist, I dreamt of starting a support group for adults suffering from OCD and anxiety disorders. There was a severe shortage of English-speaking therapists in Hong Kong when I suffered from OCD.

Little was known about this disorder, and there were no support group meetings. With encouragement from my mum and mentors along the way, I gained the confidence to run support group meetings for sufferers. The support group meetings aimed to give sufferers a safe and confidential space to share their fears and struggles without judgement.

The support group meetings were well-received, and they wanted more. This was a clear sign for me to expand mental health services to the community, to use my adversity as an opportunity to help others.

This is how OCD & Anxiety Support HK (OCDAHK), a registered mental health charity that I started, was born. It gives sufferers of mental illness support, education, advocacy, resources, and counselling services. OCDAHK has championed the green ribbon campaign, the first of its kind in Asia, to raise mental health awareness during World Mental Health Month involving corporations, schools, retailers, and NGOs. OCDAHK is a global partner of the International OCD Foundation in Boston and supports sufferers locally and internationally.

My experience with an anxiety disorder prepared me for one of the most tragic incidents that life brought me in 2016 – the sudden death of my mother. Losing her was like losing a part of me.

Without facing my fear of death, I wouldn't have been able to talk to my mum before she died about what sari she was going to wear at her funeral or where she wanted her funeral to take place, without panicking. To be at my mum's death bed, holding her and singing to her as she took her last breath, bathing her once she died and witnessing her ashes being dispersed as we bid her a final farewell was the saddest time of my life. But I wasn't scared, anxiety didn't take over, the only thing I felt was love. My mum was and will always be my biggest cheerleader.

Facing a mental health disorder requires tremendous strength and commitment, but I persevered, and I wear my battle scars proudly as it has shaped who I am today. I have recovered from OCD, but I will always experience more anxiety than the average person. I no longer shame or blame myself for it. This is who I am, and that is okay. Mental illness deserves attention, care, respect, and treatment just like a physical illness.

I am grateful for the lessons that I learnt and the knowledge that I gained from my experience which has given me the tools to serve and love others. Treatment for my anxiety disorder was a blessing, not a curse, and I encourage sufferers of mental health disorders to seek professional help. It saved my life, and I know it will impact yours too.

Remember, you are not alone. We are here to help you on your path to recovery.

About The Author

Minal Mahtani is the CEO and Founder of OCD & Anxiety Support Hong Kong, a registered mental health charity dedicated to supporting, educating, coaching and a resource to adults and teenagers who are affected by Obsessive Compulsive Disorder, Depression and Anxiety Disorders.

She is trained in Cognitive Behaviour Therapy and Acceptance Commitment Therapy and holds degrees in both Psychology and Education. She is a Mental Health First Aid Instructor and a certified Stress Management Yoga teacher.

Minal is passionate about mental health advocacy. She is the pioneer of the Green Ribbon and Stamp Out Stigma campaigns in Hong Kong, and is an integral member of the mental health community.

She is in the process of opening a counselling clinic called the Rainbow of Hope (in honour of her late mother Mira) to make mental health counselling affordable, available and accessible to all.

Minal can be contacted at:

Email: *ocdcommunityhk@gmail.com*

LinkedIn: *https://www.linkedin.com/in/mahtani-minal-69075732/*

Facebook: *https://www.facebook.com/ocdanxietyhk*

STORY FIVE

Feed Your Passion Now

I believe that you can create your own "luck". Luck is often as simple as being in the right place at the right time. Sometimes it's enough just to show up.

I was born in communist Poland, where being proactive and entrepreneurial were not highly rewarded qualities. I spent years working in corporate jobs with a line of managers and the associated hierarchy, so I am used to being a part of a big organisation.

Three years ago, without any prior small business experience I decided to start my own company. I have always been passionate about food, cooking, and health, more precisely the idea that there is a powerful link between diet and our physical and mental health.

The science behind our food has always fascinated me. There are so many "old wive's tales" about what is good for you. Many don't stand up to any real scrutiny.

To pursue my passion, I obtained certification in plant-based nutrition (from the UK, USA and Australia). This was my eureka moment. I learnt that people can truly transform their lives with healthy eating, and without expensive treatments, pills, or devices.

What you eat does matter. It has a domino effect and can change your professional life, social life, family life, and the relationships around you.

Starting with my friends, family, and colleagues I felt such a buzz when I saw that my recommendations actually helped them. The feedback I received was very encouraging. For the first time ever I felt truly fulfilled, and I got a sense of great accomplishment.

Following this revelation, I decided to share my knowledge about healthy cooking with the world. Here it was – a clear mission for my business to change the quality of life for my clients.

Unfortunately, I quickly realised it's not easy to run your own business. Immigration law (I decided to set up my company in Singapore), finance, accounting, marketing, logistics – these were all real challenges. Financially I couldn't afford to use professionals to outsource all of these tasks. I had to learn to do it myself.

At the age of 35, after many years in big corporations I had to start from scratch. I attended numerous networking events and met a lot of women in a similar situation to mine. Following their passion and dreams they wanted to set up their own businesses.

To my surprise they were working on their business plans, looking for perfect locations, ingredients, software etc. I was shocked when I heard that some of these women had spent thousands of dollars or dedicated months of their lives to find a perfect solution, having an ideal starting point. I knew straight away that was not the way to go for me.

As little girls we are often taught that everything has to be done perfectly, a spotless home, perfectly ironed linens, and polished cutlery. These ideas stop a lot of women from launching their start-ups or businesses where they can pursue their passion. Start-ups by nature are small, testing and trying, often failing on the way. It seems there are still women who are afraid of these failures.

I discovered that in order to succeed there are some things I needed to "unlearn." First was the belief that someone else is responsible for me – the "government" looking after my financial security and wellbeing, doctors and healthcare being solely responsible for my health.

Secondly, and probably more importantly, was to remove the idea that others have more luck than I have. Luck is not something we are born with, like a gift from your parents. There are a lot of stories of children of the wealthiest parents who went astray, not only did they not repeat the success of their parents, but they finished their life with alcohol/drug/gambling problems. A great example is that money and/or education doesn't guarantee success.

So, what can you do? I believe that you can create your own "luck". Luck is often as simple as being in the right place at the right time, hence if you are in more places, know more people…statistically you improve your chances to get lucky. Sometimes it's enough just to show up, get to know people from different industries or backgrounds. Find out how you can help them, and one day someone might give you a helping hand. I think that is the "formula" for getting luck in your life.

I wish to send a simple message to aspiring female entrepreneurs to focus on their strengths, not shortcomings, as all of us have some. There is a joke which says that if there is a job advertisement with five requirements and a man meets one of the five they feel that's a job for them. When a woman has four out of the five qualifications she hesitates as she doesn't feel good enough.

Unfortunately observing some women in business, I can see they are often aiming for perfection. It's great to aim for a perfect result, but sometimes it might be our blocking point. A prototype, draft, sample, or any first step achieved is more significant than a perfect plan.

Some simple advice from me, just go do it. I believe it's easier to improve or correct something. Take action today – a simple step toward your business goal. Grab a phone to make a call, or send an email to your potential customer, present your offer, idea, ask their opinion. It's great to have a five-year plan, but I think it's more important to work on small, daily goals. Those little achievements might sound insignificant, but they all are helping to create your success.

During my journey I also learnt how important our wellbeing is. For busy entrepreneurs (not only women) healthy eating should be a top priority, as the food we eat is fuel for our body and brain. That also means fuel to realise your dreams.

Changing your diet can be a first step to success in life. It can change your body and also gives you your life energy. Maybe just a kick to get up from bed and start moving.

Sometimes it is important to put yourself first, in the centre. Chasing dreams, financial goals, or annual quotas we often forget about absolute basics – proper eating, sleeping, and exercise. Eat plenty of fruits and vegetables, avoid sugar, and drink enough water. It sounds trivial, but it can really change your life.

Imagine how it feels when you wake up in the morning full of energy to fulfil a busy schedule, when you don't need to fight the afternoon slump, and evenings when you still have enough vigour to have quality time with your loved ones. The magic solution is not pills or supplements, but healthy eating habits.

Women often forget about selfcare, it's not an act of being selfish, but taking responsibility for your health. It's like the emergency procedure on a plane, you can only help other passengers when you've secured your own mask. It's the same in other areas of life, you won't be able to take care of your loved ones if you don't take care of yourself first.

On a daily basis working with both men and women I teach how important it is to look after your health. We truly are what we eat. Healthy eating is just not for celebrities or Instagrammers showing off their sixpacks.

Whether you are a busy mum, successful manager, or an important CEO you need to eat healthily as well. Simply enjoy your life, to be happy – running after or with your kids, or just waking up energised for work.

That's the important message I would like to send to all women, especially young ones, as they often think they are indestructible! Each breakfast, lunch or dinner is like an investment in your future.

Just as we invest our hard earned money into stocks, properties or commodities we should invest in our health. Dollar after dollar, you can collect a big sum, the same rules apply to your health. Meal after meal, snack after snack or drink after drink you are working on your future health. Not big steps on their own but small decisions on what we put on our plate (or most importantly what not to!) every day will build towards your health when you are 70, 80 or 90 years old.

I show my clients how to achieve the best health…and yet not compromise on flavour. I understand food is also a pleasure. But a lot of our cravings are the result of memories, learnt behaviours or traditions. Good news – we can change that! Just start with a small improvement. No step is too small. We all already know that we should cut down on fizzy drinks and fatty foods, and should try to eat a bit more fruit and vegetables.

Three years since founding my company, LivingveggiebyAnia is not exactly where I wanted it to be. I made a lot of mistakes on the way, and learnt a number of valuable lessons. I've acquired many new skills, and I believe that learning on the job is the most effective way to progress.

Fear of not being good enough stops a lot of women before they even start their own business. They are afraid they need additional qualifications, experience etc. No need to be afraid. If someone has done it before then so can you!

It took me more than a year to finally decide to set up my own business. The more research I did the more scared and overwhelmed I became. At networking events I met women with more experience than mine, on social media I saw more talented chefs than I was, I read articles by nutritionists who had more knowledge than me.

In my head, I had a plan to launch my business when my skills and experience equalled all the people I admired. Looking at this from where I am now, it was a waste of time. I could have started LivingveggiebyAnia sooner. There is always someone better than you, and you can fall into a dark place when comparing yourself to other people. You should only compare yourself with the "you" of yesterday. Try to answer the following questions honestly:

What did I learn yesterday?

How did I improve?

What can I do to improve further?

As long as you make progress (even if it's small) you are on the right track. Today both me and my company are in a better place than a year ago. I believe with hard work both will be in an even better place in a year's time.

I am convinced I will learn a lot during 2021. I believe this progress can be classified as a success. And how does it start ? With a very simple and small first step – drafting an article, sending an email or choosing a name for your business.

When you finish reading this chapter, take 15 minutes and make an action. It doesn't matter how small it seems. Anything that will bring you closer to realising your dreams. Anything that can be a start to the first chapter of your new life.

About The Author

Originally from Poland, **Ania Wojtkowska** spent a decade in Denmark after graduating with a degree in political science, before relocating to Singapore in 2013. She spent many years in corporate administration but never managed to find her true vocation.

A passionate foodie she always dreamt of swapping her busy office for a kitchen environment. To pursue this goal, she graduated from Cornell's Plant Based Nutrition by Dr Colin Campbell (USA) and plant-based nutrition from Winchester University (UK) and attended numerous cookery schools across Europe and Asia.

She now teaches the philosophy of healthy living through healthy eating at www.livingveggiebyAnia.com. She uses her nutritional knowledge in practical terms, with – cooking classes, dining events, restaurant consultations, and nutritional workshops, where she promotes the connection between diet and wellbeing.

Ania can be contacted at:

Email: ania@livingveggiebyania.com

Facebook: *https://www.facebook.com/LivingveggiebyAnia*

Instagram: *https://www.instagram.com/livingveggiebyania/*

STORY SIX

Finding Your Freedom

Have you ever been at that crossroads of what you really want and the expectations you put on yourself?

Adrenaline filled the air, and I could smell the double espressos as I entered the building at 7 am. People were already shouting across the trading floor.

I could taste the tension as I walked through the doors, bracing myself for the volatile day ahead. My head was hoping for an escape route, and my heart was withdrawing from my current reality. My body was calling out for me to stop. I had suffered debilitating back pain since being on the trading desk. But every day, I coaxed myself into thinking strong thoughts, being disciplined to get through each day, fighting the threshold for what I could handle.

My years as a derivatives trader made me withdraw further into my shell, numb from the external stresses and daily pressures I faced. When the alarm rang every morning, I would begin my internal pep talk, "You can do this, just get out of bed; today will be a good day." And every moment from the time I got out of bed, I was yearning to go back to the comfort of my blanket, where I could switch my mind off and feel safe.

Why was it that in my early twenties, I was always exhausted? What made me feel so disconnected from my existence? I was earning great money, and I had graduated from one of the world's top universities. I had a prestigious career in an international investment bank with the promise of a bright future. So, why did I feel so small, so insignificant? Why was life so meaningless? Here I was struggling with my sense of purpose. How was I to help others? I knew I had to make a difference to others. I needed to begin a serious quest to help myself.

I carried on with the job. My satisfaction and motivation were at rock bottom. I suffered from burnout, didn't have the energy to do the smallest of tasks, my attention was compromised, and my performance declined. During the global financial crisis, it was no surprise that I was made redundant. I didn't leave my job, my job left me. Having my severance package in hand and freedom from a role that drained me, I felt a deep relief walking out the office doors for the very last time.

I was grateful that this decision was made for me because I didn't have the courage to make it myself. I was so attached to the image of being a "high flying young banker", I couldn't say "I give up". I was so worried about what others would think if I quit.

Have you ever been at that crossroads of what you really want and the expectations you put on yourself? I was bothered more about what others thought that I hid how I really felt. What does this lead to? A lot of suppressed tension and emotion that over time manifests in ill health. The physical pain, the listless sleep, constant indigestion, and inflammation were alarms that could no longer go unattended. The more I ignored them, the louder they got.

So, who are these "others" whose opinions I regarded so highly? I realised those who care about me are always there to support what I believe in. Chasing validation creates self-loathing within yourself.

Social recognition became the core of my identity, which made me feel trapped. It reinforced the notion that I was not good enough, that I needed to comply and conform to be accepted. It makes us operate from our ego, behind thick walls of separateness stuck in the formal exchange transaction.

Taking this leap of faith to serve others helped me feel a deep sense of belonging with myself, rejoicing in the action that sprung from a sense of compassion. It had meaning and purpose, and it was the first time I felt energised and uplifted by the work itself. I have followed through with projects that feel true to myself, where my heart is in it, whether socially or professionally. It brings a zest, sincerity, and joy to the work and upholds a deep sense of responsibility much more than sheer willpower could get me through.

Call it coincidence or Divine timing, a week before getting laid off, my yoga teacher took me aside after class and said, "Neelam, you've been practicing for 12 years now… there's not much more I can teach you. You are ready to become a teacher now."

I was so humbled that he thought I could qualify to teach others. Being practical, I thought, "I wish, but I can't quit my day job." I was presented with a situation that I secretly wished for but didn't dare to control. Since I was not prepared to do it myself, the opportunity was given to me. In hindsight, I viewed this moment as an opportunity.

Most of our challenges are opportunities to grow, right? We view them as a crisis at the time, but surely the circumstance pushes us to reach new heights when we are ready for a transformation. Rising to new possibilities is akin to a butterfly squeezing out of its cocoon. Breaking free from a limitation it imposed onto itself, metamorphosis takes place, but that doesn't mean it's easy or comfortable. I was no longer a banker, but that did not make me any less of a person. I decided to listen to what made me truly happy rather than live up to a false image of myself.

This shedding of my false identity brought me an incredible lightness. Finding freedom as you lose the idea that a role defines you. No matter how many roles we play, it's limiting. Each of these roles comes with some set of implicit rules; how we *should* behave, what's right and wrong. This moves us away from our natural essence. Years of meditation have helped me create space within myself to witness the roles that I play. All the thoughts that swirl around, all the judgments that I carry. I come back to meditation as a place to clear and let go of all the expectations. It's in this space where we can reset, recalibrate and restore.

Having left banking, my next career step was ambiguous. There was no epiphany to pivot into wellness. I simply said yes to the invitation to join the yoga teacher training program that summer and was open to the possibilities thereafter. I loved the course, and teaching felt authentic and natural to me. It finally clicked. I wanted to reach out to more to join my classes, and this was before the dawn of social media. My marketing method was as basic as sticking simple homemade posters around my local neighbourhood that read "Free Yoga Class, every weekday 9-10 am."

Things evolved quickly and a small group formed. Some days 1-2 people attended, others there were up to 12 people. But sure enough, every day, I showed up, did my best, and it felt amazing. I fell in love with teaching yoga. This ability to rescue my students from their own minds, to enjoy this very moment was so refreshing. I could see a clear result from my effort, with smiles on my students' faces after each class. It felt so right.

It all started with free classes – so there was a much deeper operating system at work. This was happiness. For the first time, I wasn't putting an "if…then…" limitation to my inner state. If I *fill in the blank* then I will be happy.

Don't we all do this? We acknowledge that everything we do is with the motive to be happy, the marriage, the divorce, the bank balance, the physique, and yet is happiness really there? When we look for happiness externally, it's governed by the law of diminishing marginal utility.

I use my services as a gateway to go inward, to transcend the fleeting pleasures, and tap into the lasting joy. We spend our entire lives entangled in this search, but when do we really give ourselves permission to feel happy? This is only available at the present moment. If we aren't happy now, the moment is wasted, isn't it? Once we connect to that *process* of experiencing the joy right now and not the elusive outcome of postponed happiness, then this is what it means to be truly alive.

The journey from teaching yoga to having a professional team of instructors to being a corporate wellness ambassador blossomed without any architectural blueprints. How did it all come to grow organically? Was it all luck? I've pondered this for years. Looking back, it's now clear that I was acting from a place of joy, growth, and awareness of the present. I was just focusing on how to create a greater impact at that moment.

People would come to me for different objectives, but it was clear the unifying thread was freedom from stress. I knew that there was no one size fits all package and that the magic lay in personalisation.

I focused on the individual and taught exclusive private classes. I wanted to bring lasting transformation and not just the acrobatics of advanced asana. I know each person holds tension in different places of the body, and in order to optimise energy, I work closely with breath awareness.

My students were touched by the sincerity of service and were passionate about seeing my business thrive. They referred me to multiple networks of friends, connected me to HR directors of multinational organisations, and put me on stage to share my message. There was so much demand, I trained a team of teachers, knowing if I want to grow my impact, I had to share my techniques.

Together we have now taught thousands of classes, all with the same vision of garnering self-love because this is what truly heals. Ironically I spend most of my time with highly driven corporate employees, propagating the message of prevention, self-awareness, optimising energy, embodying balance and resilience from stress. I am able to stand before them as a rehabilitated veteran of burnout on the battleground.

The worldwide lockdown caused by Coronavirus, stirred something deep within me. I knew I could do more to help. Having arrived back in Hong Kong from India with both my children at the precipice of the global pandemic, I spent two weeks in quarantine. When I felt anxious, panicked, and fearful from all the uncertainty, I found myself gravitating back to my yoga mat to find my centre. I was overwhelmed with gratitude for my personal toolkit to feel stable and calm. I realised I had a precious gift.

While the majority of people were dealing with their mental health, I could come back to find my centre, naturally and on my own. It was the gift of self-practice.

I realised I had a gift of easing mental, emotional, and physical struggles to share with the world.

That's when I turned my son's nursery into a home studio and filmed the entire nine week online program "From Stress to Success" in 21 hours. This was my time to act. This program has solidified a self-practice in so many around the world, and it was my conviction to help that pushed me out of my comfort zone and in front of the camera in dedication to what I care so deeply about.

My actions are firmly rooted in the intention to help others and feel joy with the work we can do. Have you gone through hardship or great challenges when at the time, you were devastated, but in retrospect, it was the best thing that could've happened to you? These turning points are the defining moments for us to grow, expand our horizons, and blossom from strength to strength.

About The Author

Neelam Harjani is the founder of Inspire Yoga, operating in Hong Kong since 2011 with a vision of "providing an antidote for fast paced city life" through personalised onsite programs of yoga and mindfulness.

In Hong Kong Neelam has been invited to counsel government statutory and advisory bodies in wellness, female empowerment and multicultural inclusion.

Previously an investment banker, she structures her mind-body paradigms with science and experience, taking an integrative approach to release occupational tension and connect with holistic health, physical, mental and emotional.

Having more than 20 years of experience in yoga, Neelam has formulated a system that draws attention to our intentions, launching the "Transforming Stress to Success" online learning course to provide support to the global community amidst COVID-19.

Her journey and somatic techniques have been published on SCMP and Asian Entrepreneur highlighting personal anecdotes of how a shift in mindset releases suppressed tightness and delivers tremendous energy in her clients.

Neelam can be contacted at:

Email: *neelam@inspire-yoga.com*

Website: *www.inspire-yoga.com*

LinkedIn: *https://www.linkedin.com/in/neelam-harjani/*

STORY SEVEN

From Judgement to Acceptance

Judgement (of any sort) has created every issue and limiting belief that we cultivate, and the only route to freedom is to accept what we have judged before.

As a young girl, I craved acceptance and was overly concerned with people's opinions of me. I lived with the illusion that I had a say about people's perceptions and thought that the route to my happiness would be to change my behaviour to match societal ideals.

Whilst altering my exterior did make a difference to my self-perception, it was temporary and didn't generate the inner confidence I'd hoped for. Moreover, I realised that I couldn't predict what was acceptable to others because I'm not a mind-reader, and to make it more challenging, people's opinions keep changing!

I gathered very early on that the biggest source of my dissatisfaction were my own beliefs. I was my biggest critic and was putting crazy conditions on myself just so that I could feel good about myself! This was an enlightening realisation that came to me gradually, starting from my teens.

I didn't have a single moment of epiphany but a series of defining events that made me more aware of my thoughts. One such event was during a school trip in my teens where we were taken to McDonald's for lunch, something that excited every kid except me. My lack of enthusiasm was not for health reasons but because I felt conscious of speaking up and ordering my meal in front of all the others.

It sounds so trivial now and even ironic for someone who is now a professional speaker. But back then, I felt so concerned about what other people would think about the way I spoke that I drove myself to a point where I just couldn't talk. When I got to the front of the line, the girl behind me had to decode my whispers and order my meal for me!

That experience was one I never wanted to have again. At first, I blamed myself for not being confident enough. Later I began to question *why* I wasn't confident and what made me so overly concerned about people's opinions.

It's this questioning that marked the turning point for me. It's easy to make statements blaming ourselves for not being enough, but the moment we ask ourselves *why*, our mind searches for how to answer that question, which leads to some pretty profound realisations.

My curiosity took me on an inner journey to understand where my beliefs came from. Right as I graduated from university, I subjected myself to a plethora of books, courses, and training so that I could understand how beliefs are created, what makes them so powerful, and how to alter them so that they could serve instead of sabotage me. This learning has taken place over the last 15 years, and I am still on this journey, as evolution is an ongoing process.

My quest led me to study human behaviour, studying got me qualifications, and those qualifications eventually lead me to a full-blown career as a practitioner and owner of a wellness centre. I have trained in various modalities, including Life Coaching, Hypnotherapy, Image Consulting, Systemic Constellation, NLP, Reiki, Sekhem, Chakra Healing, Counselling, and Transpersonal Regression Therapy.

Right from the beginning, people were naturally drawn to me and asked me to practice what I was learning on them. When I saw them going through shifts in their self-esteem, my conviction in my work grew, and I knew that this is what I am meant to be doing. My work grew organically, starting with a few sessions to a growing clientele, to opening a training institute to teach people to do what I do, to setting up a wellness centre, and eventually to designing my own courses and writing a book.

Through all my years of introspection, the main message I've gained is that judgement (of any sort) has created every issue and limiting belief that we cultivate, and the only route to freedom is to *accept* what we have judged before. It may sound simple, but it takes a high level of awareness.

True healing only happens from within. *We* are the only ones who can create shifts for ourselves, and this is an ongoing journey for everyone. The truth is that we have always been "enough."

We moved away from this truth very early on when we were introduced to judgements, comparisons, and given benchmarks of the way things should be. All this made us feel like there is something wrong with us, and we developed coping mechanisms to try and cover it up or prove otherwise. It's only when we are in enough pain (as I was) that we finally can let go of the layers of judgement and discover that we have always been enough, and judgements are a figment of our own ignorant interpretations.

Conscious living is not about changing negative beliefs into positive ones. It's much deeper than that. If you think about it, both negative and positive are forms of judgements and need each other to exist. Conscious living is about moving out of judgement altogether and towards being at peace with "what is."

It took me a while to truly understand this, as I initially went into personal development with an attitude to "fix" myself, as many people do. I was feeling unaccomplished and inferior, and I thought that I just needed to reprogram myself to feel the opposite – capable and superior. Little did I know that this only started one of the journeys but was not my answer to the eternal happiness I thought I wanted.

Step one is the most crucial step to any journey, and for me, it was about moving from victimhood to knowing that I have the power to change something in my world. When we are victims, we feel like things are done to us, and we have no responsibility. We all have victim stories about how something "*always* happens to us."

My victim narrative was that my voice doesn't deserve to be heard, and others are more valuable than me. And because I believed it, it was true! As I changed my narrative to be more deserving, my behaviour changed, and I became more expressive. I could speak up for myself and realised how much I actually enjoyed it. I had found my voice, I was confident to express it, and I saw that people were benefiting from listening to what I had to say. I began to take part in plays and radio shows, hosted events, and volunteered to take roles where I could speak about my learnings.

This felt really good, and for a long time, I was on a high until I realised that I had a hidden expectation to *feel good permanently*. When I had moments of sadness or anger, I would tell myself that "after all this inner-work, how can I still feel sad or down?" The more I told myself off, the more it persisted, and this was how step two began to reveal itself.

My next big learning was to understand that I will be experiencing highs and lows no matter *how much* inner-work I do. It's part of life, and I can resist it or be with it. This was when I began to understand the difference between beliefs and emotions. I had the power to shift my beliefs, but certain emotions are innate that I judged as negative, and I would continue to experience them, namely fear, anger, and sadness.

I noticed that even newborn babies and animals feel these emotions, so it must be a natural response to certain situations. It's natural to feel scared when our life is threatened, or to feel angry when our boundaries are violated, or to feel sad when we lose something, and it's okay to feel that way! It took a high level of awareness for me to allow myself to experience these emotions when I felt them, and in doing so, I was naturally accepting that I was feeling them. I felt a great sense of liberation to allow myself to just *experience* what I was feeling.

I was moving away from all those rules of how I *should* be and how I was *supposed* to feel, to just accepting how I am feeling. What a relief that was! I allowed myself to express my feelings, not by suppressing or exploding, but by sharing. I got that we are on an emotional journey where we will continue to feel a whole spectrum of emotions, judging will only suppress what's already there, and accepting allows it to move and be complete.

Again, I felt like I had made another fundamental shift in my journey, and removed more layers of judgement. Just before it translated into an ego-boost, I was humbled by another self-realisation when I saw how disappointed I got when people didn't see what I saw. I was expecting other people to be as accepting towards my feelings as I was. This marked the beginning of step three, and the final big step of my evolution.

I was assuming people would be as accepting of my emotions as I was learning to be myself. I unconsciously expected them to understand how I was honouring my innate emotions and expressing them as a way to practice acceptance, which I had recently discovered.

Of course, they didn't do that. People in my life were echoing my previous beliefs of needing to be perfectly compiled all the time now that I was a practicing therapist. Sometimes it would look like friends asking me how come I am at peace all the time, which presupposes I am, and if I wasn't, they would consider that fraudulent.

My biggest lesson here was getting that no matter what I do or say, I don't have 100% control over other people's thoughts and feelings.

Judgement will continue to exist (in me and others), and I need to accept that. Even if I am learning to accept myself and life more, they may choose to judge, and I need to *accept that*! Accepting other people's unacceptance was a big one for me. It taught me the meaning of mindfulness all over again. I understood that acceptance is not about agreeing with something or feeling resigned to it. It's about getting that things are the way they are, and it doesn't mean anything about us. People are not going to be the way we want them to be all the time, and that's *their* journey; it's not about us, and there's nothing we can do about that.

My major lessons have been:

1. Recognising that our behaviour is influenced by our beliefs, our beliefs have been created by us, and we have the power to shift our reality by changing our debilitating beliefs.

2. Understanding that no state is constant. No matter how much inner work we do, we will go through ups and downs in life, and we will feel emotional highs and lows. It's a part of life, and we need to allow ourselves to feel fully.
3. Accepting that judgement exists within people, and that's okay. The only aspect of life that we have full control over is our own beliefs, choices, and actions. We can inspire others but cannot change them. The only way we can be at peace is to accept what is and keep moving.

To sum up, we are all on a learning journey that never ends. Every footstep that we take can replay an old story or create a new reality for us. It is inevitable for us to face judgement and fall along the way, and when that happens, we have the choice to learn from it. Life will keep throwing surprises at us. If we find ourselves in a place we don't want to be, all we need to do is accept where we are, express ourselves authentically, keep moving forward, and check what we've learned along the way. All this is a part of learning the lesson of acceptance.

About The Author

Sonia Samtani is Founder and CEO of All About You, a leading mental wellness centre in Hong Kong offering therapy, training, workshops, and personalised healing products. She is a licensed Clinical Hypnotherapist and Hypnotherapy instructor, NLP Trainer, Life Coach, Corporate Trainer, Family Constellation Facilitator, Regression Therapist, and Public Speaking Coach.

As a sought-after mental health expert and public speaker, Sonia has been leading workshops since 2005, and has designed several programs to facilitate deep healing and conscious living. Sonia has spoken twice on the TEDx platform, and has been featured in Vogue, Tatler, Cosmopolitan, TimeOut, Jessica and MarieClaire. At the end of 2020 Sonia launched her book called *52 thoughts for Conscious Living.*

Sonia's vision is to empower individuals with simple, yet powerful tools to navigate through the ups and downs of life with acceptance, so that they can tune into the magnificence of who they are.

Sonia can be contacted at:

Email: *sonia@soniasamtani.com*

LinkedIn: *https://www.linkedin.com/in/soniasamtani/*

Website: *https://www.allaboutyoucentre.com/*

STORY EIGHT

From Rescue Me to Resilient Me

What I learnt that day is that we have the power in us — the power to choose.

All my childhood, I waited for a superhero. Someone who would save my family and me from all the challenges we were going through. As I grew up, I realised that heroes existed only in books and movies.

It was International Women's Day, 2018. Enrique Iglesias was playing in the background, and I was touching up my lipstick, mentally rehearsing the speech I was about to give when the phone rang. I answered the phone with a smile on my face that rapidly turned into a look of fear. It was the call that changed my life and became the origin story for discovering my superpower.

When I got that call four years ago, my heart sank. It was from a victim of domestic abuse. After enduring thirty years of torment, her husband had thrown her out of the house in the middle of the night. She lived in an extremely unsafe part of town where someone could get mugged in broad daylight. The nights were equally terrifying – green flora around the broken home blanketed her vision with only the flickering of half-hearted dim streetlights to keep her company. She had no place to go, slept on the cold, hard floor, crying and fearing for her life. Waiting for the first rays of the morning sun, she took the first chance she had to hurry back inside and call me.

She recounted her experience as I stood frozen, unsure of how to react.

The woman – was my mother.

Here I was on one side of the world, excited to deliver a talk on empowerment to a room full of successful women. Meanwhile, on the other side of the world stood the woman who gave me life, unsure of when she would feel safe again.

I wanted to scream. I wanted to pray. I wanted to take the next flight and rescue her, but she refused. At that moment, I realised something I didn't think was possible.

She didn't want to be rescued, now or ever.

That's when I wanted to give up. On everything. How does someone go on knowing their mother has accepted that she'll live in her home like a prisoner, trapped in a cage of thirty long years of bruises and insults from their captor. Nothing made sense. I fought back my tears and decided to hold strong. I presented at the women's empowerment event and came home to give my dad an ultimatum.

The next day I didn't dare face the world and planned to spend the day hiding in bed, but the phone rang again. It wasn't my mother but a friend, someone who relied on my advice and support. And just like that, I was re-energised. My friend and I talked deeply and for hours, ending the call with fresh perspectives and a new sense of optimism and confidence, and it dawned on me what I was always meant to do. I finally understood that it was my life's purpose to help women. My superpower was resilience.

If I wasn't going to be able to help my mom, at least I could continue to use my new-found sense of resilience to help women in similar situations. I could actively utilise my adversity as a strength instead of spending my days in a negative, depressed state, ruminating on a situation I had no control over. Resilience is a choice. To get up and feel motivated, strengthening your ability to move on no matter the circumstance. What I learnt that day is that we have the power in us — the power to choose.

After that epiphany, there was no stopping me. At that time, I was at a point in my career exploring a transition from healthcare management. I joined a mentoring program and started guiding young women from challenging backgrounds.

My work with a non-profit organization also opened my eyes to the grave struggles faced by women from various industries. I realised that they were losing their sense of identity during the journey of fighting life's challenges and gradually slipping into depression. According to WHO, by 2030, depression will be the single leading cause of disability globally.

Back home, my best friend, who was incredibly smart and full of life, struggled with no way to escape from a narcissistic husband, and I felt helpless. I yearned to help her. It felt as if I was fighting against the world all by myself. This yearning to help such women became much stronger in me, and I joined a coaching program to get certified as a coach.

During the program, the first coachee was a woman going through relationship challenges and abuse. Initially, it was excruciatingly tough not to be reminded of my mom's struggles. But gradually with each session, I got stronger, wiser, and resilience started overriding my sense of helplessness. And the sense of gratification I felt after seeing the transformation in my clients from a helpless, oppressed individual to a more confident woman was the highlight of my coaching journey.

I decided then that I will not let any adversity define me, and I refuse to be reduced by it. I started focusing on choosing better, and with each challenge, I started getting more resilient. This helped me coach women in my community to recognise that our trauma affects each of us differently. Yet, the difference between the calm and the panicked, is their decision to use their resilience to strengthen themselves and mend the cracks. I started looking forward to interacting with women from various walks of life every day, guiding them towards uncovering their hidden superpower — resilience. We can choose to rescue ourselves.

What happens during a crisis? When something adverse and unexpected happens, we get stressed, worried, anxious about the uncertainty. We go into a victim mindset. Even without a crisis, our mind is cluttered with thoughts of our everyday life, so once adversity happens, it only exacerbates it.

How can we stay calm and make good choices during a crisis? Looking back, I tried to understand what helped me maintain my sanity and strength throughout these difficulties.

Knowing that my mother's situation is an experience shared by many women, I have formulated the **ART Framework** to guide the choices in resilience we make when we are trapped in adversity.

The **ART Framework** consists of the following three ways of choosing resilience during a crisis. They can be used by anyone.

A – ACCEPTANCE. Whenever a crisis hits, we tend to think of the worst-case scenario, and our brain goes into panic mode. Why does this happen? Why does the smartest organ in the human body, which is the seat of intelligence, do this as a first reaction? Research shows that our brains evolved to react more strongly to negative experiences than positive ones. It's what used to keep us safe from danger during caveman days. However, we can't continue in this panicked state and give up. Whenever we are in that state, the first thing to do is calm ourselves by taking some slow deep breaths. After that, ask yourself:

Can I control this situation in any way? If the answer is yes, then think of ways of making it better. But, if the answer is no, try to make some sense of it and accept the reality knowing that nothing is under your control.

Once you make the decision that this is not in your control, **accept reality**. It is what it is. You can only change your thoughts about it before the situation spins out of control. Our brain is constantly seeking connections to form meaning. It needs some explanation or reasoning to make sense of what's happening. After accepting the situation, you're in the right state to move forward.

Choose to accept reality, don't resist it.

R – RE-FRAMING. It refers to seeing the current situation from a different perspective. It involves identifying our negative thoughts and replacing them with more positive adaptive ones. However, we often underestimate just how powerful our minds really are. We can always choose to **re-frame** our negative thoughts, looking at the crisis from a different perspective. Once you have accepted this reality, ask yourself:

What is the best way to see the crisis in front of you? Ok. This crisis happened, but it's not in my control, so how can I look at it differently so it doesn't impact every aspect of my life? The realisation that we choose how we think about the crisis is very empowering, and that sets the stage for our next step.

Choose to re-frame your situation.

T – TAKING ACTION. Once we accept the reality and re-frame our perspective about the crisis, then we can start thinking about our action plan.

What can we do to get to a better state? Either we choose to get over the crisis and have a solid plan on how to move on with life, or think of ways to manage the crisis to get to a better state. As you know, life is 10% of what happens to us and 90% of how we respond. We have to choose carefully where we are putting our focus and attention because energy flows where focus goes.

Choose to take action.

Resilience is a Choice

People often ask me, "Is resilience a trait you're born with or a state of mind you develop?" The world's top resilience expert Dr. Rick Hanson says one-third of it is in our DNA, and two-thirds is how we develop it and become more resilient with every challenge we face.

In life's journey, we will have our highs and lows. Some days we will be full of energy and enthusiasm, but other days we will feel drained and negative. Always hold on to hope and optimism. Keep building your strong inner core by accepting, adapting, and building your resilience in every crisis. Nothing inspires me more than seeing women rise up to face their adversities.

What can we do to practice building resilience daily? Try to embrace change – see change as a learning opportunity, accept it and learn how to manage it. Be optimistic about life and when things go wrong, re-frame your mindset. Mindfulness – connect with the inner self by doing yoga or meditation or just sitting with ourselves and doing something we enjoy.

Resilience Mantra

"This too will pass. It's not going to last forever." This has always been my ***resilience mantra.*** So, what is yours? An empowering belief which keeps you going during a challenging situation. If you don't have one yet, don't worry. There's an easy exercise you can do to find yours! Think back to a time in your life when you have gone through a crisis, and then try and recall what belief of yours pulled you through that time. That is your resilience mantra! This mantra will bring you hope and optimism through challenging times. Above all, show self-compassion. Acknowledge that you are doing your best, and be grateful. Gradually allow yourself to move from a victim to a survivor mindset. Choose to rise and don't give up.

Identify at least three strong friends who can be your ***pillars of strength*** and pull you up to catch your breath at times when you are drowning.

Adversities in life are inevitable. What we don't realise is that we all have the power to rescue ourselves. There is no superhero required. It's just you and your superpower – the power to choose to be resilient.

Create your mantra and take back your life

"Don't be defined by your traumatic past, reduced by your adverse present, or fearful about your uncertain future. Break free from all those labels and create your brand new past, present, and future by re-framing your narrative ."

During any crisis, you can choose to be resilient. The choice is always yours.

About The Author

Neetha Sanjay is an International Coach Federation (ICF) Certified Life and Career Coach who is passionate about empowering women to achieve their life and career goals.

A dental surgeon by training, with more than a decade of experience in healthcare management, Neetha enjoys sharing her learning by speaking on confidence, resilience, and positivity and helping women advance their lives and careers.

By powering through her own adversities and career transitions, she is determined to spread the message of courage, "Be brave and travel your own road, and if there's none, then pave one for yourself."

Being an advocate for women, Neetha is committed to working with organizations that help uplift the next generation of female leaders, focusing on those from underserved communities.

She is also a community leader for the elderly and women through her various leadership roles at Sree Narayana Mission and other non-profit organizations.

Neetha can be contacted at:

Email: *neethasconsulting@gmail.com*

LinkedIn: *https://www.linkedin.com/in/neetha-sanjay-life-coach*

Facebook: *https://www.facebook.com/NeethaSanjayConsulting/*

STORY NINE

Greatest Gift of Giving – Inclusion

Small acts of humanity and humility should be instilled in children from a young age - It is our way of telling that life is worth more than the marks they score while studying and the money they earn at work.

"An individual has not started living until he can rise above the narrow confines of his individualistic concerns to the broader concerns of all humanity."

—Martin Luther King, Jr.

I grew up in a family that taught me to dream big and then work to achieve those dreams. While growing up, the spirit of giving was instilled in me very early on in life by my parents. I watched them volunteer, not just with money, but with their time and their hearts. They taught me that true philanthropy was about action, making things happen, and about actually getting involved.

I studied Engineering and followed that up with a Master degree in Financial Engineering & Risk Management from New York University. This focus on STEM and Economics enabled me to think rationally and universally – ensuring I understood how to deploy the finances at my disposal for maximum productiveness.

Soon after graduating, I joined my family's thriving jewellery business, but I always made sure to constantly be in touch with the charities my parents and I supported, contributing financially from afar and visiting them in person in India whenever I had the opportunity.

Life changed a bit when my husband, Gaurav, and I decided to move to Hong Kong for business expansion.

While it was initially challenging moving from New York, our home for so long, Hong Kong soon felt like home too.

Though my circumstances and experiences were new, my interest in poverty alleviation always remained the same. What I had experienced and seen as a child shaped me as an adult, and those lessons never wavered. I did a lot of reading, learning, and unlearning to understand why people get caught in a poverty trap. It became apparent that it is impossible to break the cycle of poverty if people aren't healthy and educated. And that's where my journey of working at the grassroots level began.

With my daughters getting older, I wanted to start devoting more time to work and contributing to the society I lived in. That is how I started to work with the Sarjan Charity Foundation (SCF).

I joined the Foundation Committee and later went on to be elected Chairperson for four years. This role allowed me to have constant encounters with new and passionate people working for the causes they believe in, selflessly and tirelessly. This has been a blessing for me. They have been a ceaseless source of inspiration.

But of all the lessons in life that have kept me motivated, the most important one has to do with my elder daughter, Tanisha, who was then an incredibly compassionate eight-year-old. When I told her about doing our first food drive in Hong Kong, she was super excited and immediately got to work planning how to reach out to everyone she knew, everyone her parents knew, and most importantly, reaching out to people we didn't know.

She taught me to dare, to not stop and hesitate. She managed to raise 1200 meals a day herself. She did all that with only eight years of life experience and resources. It made me realise what all I could achieve by channelling my own resources.

Since then, she has been proactively helping me in my humble efforts. She accompanied me to one of the artificial limb fitting camps we support – it was her first such experience as a ten-year-old. She was overwhelmed at seeing hundreds of disabled people together, obviously a shock for any young child.

That day she taught me one of my life's biggest lessons, that "Courage is not always a roar. Sometimes courage is the little voice at the end of the day that says I'll try again tomorrow" in the words of Mary Anne Radmacher.

Even at that tender age, she knew that while we couldn't solve every problem for everyone, we had to solve the problems we could. This is how our relationship has developed and strengthened.

We accompany each other to old-age homes, providing the elderly with medicines, quilts, meals, and reading to them. While I give her company, she quietly gives me strength, motivation, and a steady stream of inspiration.

Since visiting our first camp in India, we've significantly increased our efforts to provide prosthetics to those who have lost a leg/hand to accidents and disease. We've set up three artificial limb fitting camps in India.

Bhagwan Mahaveer Viklang Sahayata Samiti (BMVSS), founded by Mr. D.R. Mehta is one of the world's largest free artificial limb fitting organisations. Having the privilege to hold camps with BMVSS across India and fitting more than 1100 disabled individuals (so far) with one or more artificial limbs, and providing them with wheelchairs and tricycles has been one of the most moving experiences of my life. Enabling a person to walk is giving them an equal opportunity to meet new challenges. It is not only making an individual independent but their family independent as well.

These small acts of humanity and humility should be instilled in our children from a young age at home and in our schools. It is our way of telling the next generation that life is worth more than the marks they score while studying and the money they earn at work.

The first step to doing that is telling them what it means to have the privilege. It is extremely important for parents to teach financial wisdom to their own children in a practical way that will help them their whole lives.

Teaching our children three basic tenets when it comes to money – saving, spending, and giving, is invaluable. Giving is equally important to saving and spending. This is a profound lesson in showing them that no matter how young or old, everyone can make a difference if they want to!

After my initial years of working with organisations helping developmentally challenged kids with disabilities like Cerebral Palsy, ADHD, Down syndrome, Autism, etc., I realised the families of these children also feel a lot of psychological trauma because their children are not able to integrate with other "normal" school kids.

The daily routines of these families are extremely busy, including not only normal daily life but also the provision of extra occupational therapy or speech therapy or physical exercises or simply care at home to help them develop. It is not one person who is impacted but the whole family.

For this reason, I also became associated with the Cafe Project of Hong Chi Morning Hope School, which we partially funded. It was an extremely rewarding association. The Cafe caters as a training centre to students with mild developmental delays.

It was a moving experience to see the precision and skills the graduating class developed in preparing an array of vegan snacks and lemonade, coffee and tea for all the visiting guests after only a few months of training. The cherry on top was having a few of the graduates find jobs in other cafes despite COVID-19.

There was such a thrill in seeing these students getting paid for the first time. There was so much pride and joy shown by their parents who were able to see their children become financially independent and integrating into society. It was both humbling and satisfying at the same time.

Another long-cherished association has been with an organisation called Watchdog, which works with children under six years of age with developmental challenges. Watchdog provides various therapies like speech, occupational, musical, etc. In this association of more than six years we have funded their libraries for educational, fine, and gross motor skill development. It has been an amazing journey for me to see how a little effort and the commitment of teachers to the children and their families has brought big changes in their developing brains.

By interacting with a host of well-intentioned people on this journey, I have realised having a dream and making it work are two different things. I've ensured transparency in my work, focused on keeping costs to a minimum, encouraged people to contribute their time *pro bono*, and collaborated with different organisations that had similar goals. I am grateful for the support of my family, my colleagues and the people who have contributed both as volunteers and financially because without them, it wouldn't have been possible to make as big a difference as we do!

Most importantly, the biggest outcome and end goal for pursuing all these activities is INCLUSION. Sometimes the greatest gift one can give another is to simply include them.

Working for children with special needs made me understand the depth of my own strength, tenacity, and resourcefulness. We have taught our children that not everyone has the same skills, abilities or opportunities.

When my second daughter, Sophie, turned eight, she had her beautiful long hair cut, to donate to a charity making wigs for cancer-affected children. Although she does miss putting on her hair ties, she doesn't complain because she knows someone needier than herself will be cherishing her hair dearly.

During my journey, I've often wondered, "Do my actions matter? Have they had an actual impact?" But those questions were self-limiting beliefs talking.

I learnt, all you must do is take that leap of faith and not focus on the result.

I also learnt that everyone's experience is unique. You don't have to be perfect to give back to your community. All you need is the right intent and the self-belief required to embrace what you have to offer.

Diversity is a fact, but inclusion is an act. Inclusion should be promoted at home, in schools, and in the workplace. And my belief has only gotten stronger through the years because of my family. My husband is my cheerleader and champion, my in-laws are the best coaches a person could ask for.

Through my philanthropic experiences I have developed the opinion that teachers should be trained to teach students with diverse needs and learning styles and promote a positive learning environment. This will help children treat their differently abled peers as equals. It will encourage them to see a person first and their disability later. If we can teach our children empathy and to value diversity, they will build more meaningful friendships, becoming better citizens, employees and partners in life.

People often ask what led to my decision to dedicate so much of my time and energy to *pro bono* philanthropy. The truth is, I always believed that helping make the world a better place would be an integral part of my existence – because that is how my parents raised me.

About The Author

Sonal D. Nigam is a perfectionist, businesswoman, philanthropist, mother of two awesome daughters, wife to a businessman with a passion for golf. She is determined to live life by her own rules, and is a firm believer in the power of Karma.

Brought up by her humble educationist parents who were always there to help the community, Sonal strongly believes in family bonds, discipline, steadfast ethics and moral beliefs. She believes that these traits come from a deep emphasis on education, sports, charity, dreaming big and working hard to achieve those dreams.

One of Sonal's biggest passions is striving to make a difference in the lives of others who are forgotten by our busy world.

Sonal grew up in India, pursued her higher education in New York. She worked with her husband, Gaurav, for more than a decade in New York City, before moving halfway across the world to Hong Kong. Her life is full of adventures and new beginnings.

Sonal can be contacted at:

Email: *darbarisonal@gmail.com*

STORY TEN

Having Faith

You never know the ending may be the beginning of a new journey.

I grew up in the beautiful city of Islamabad in Pakistan. Though I belonged to a family of lawyers, my decision to study medicine came from my nurturing and compassionate nature.

Soon after completing my MBBS, I married the man of my dreams at the young age of 22. I became the mother of two beautiful children who are the apples of my eye.

Willingly and happily, I sacrificed my dreams and ambitions to be the perfect loyal housewife and devoted mother. Life was a fairytale!

But fifteen years on, things changed. While I was busy raising a wonderful family, the bubble of my perfect life burst. My husband left me for greener pastures.

I was devastated! Left to raise two young children and run a household on my own. Completely shattered, I wanted to hide. I wanted to be buried in Mother Earth, or be raised to the skies to find shelter from the agony caused by the betrayal. What came next were sleepless nights, insecurity, and disbelief. I sank to a level where I thought I was not good enough. I considered myself a failed version of my former self.

I begged Allah to guide me. When I visited Khana Kabba my prayers were answered. It was a life-changing experience that gave me a new determination and a new sense of direction. I knew I had to manage my emotions and think straight. I went for counselling that helped me a lot. I was able to think about myself, my future, and move my life in the right direction.

Despite the apparent catastrophe and the worst nightmare that a woman like me could have, I refused to give up and surrender. I stood up to rebuild my empire and destiny. I gathered the broken pieces of my heart and my life and moulded myself into the most precious jewel I was always destined to be.

Hurt made me resilient; indeed, it was a blessing in disguise. Mother Nature gave me a second chance to prove my strength and become a symbol of women's empowerment. I saw the true colours of people I considered very close. But I was again on a road where I had stopped expecting from others because expectations lead to disappointment. Rebuilding wasn't easy, but I was focused.

For years, I had ignored myself. I prioritised others over me. Now, I was determined to improve my physical and mental well-being. But achieving this wasn't easy.

I still remember the pain I had to endure when I fell on my tailbone while exercising. I had a hairline fracture of my coccyx. I was advised to rest, but again if I had rested who would drive my children to school? I didn't want to miss work, as I desperately needed the income at the time.

When I look back, it gives me a lot of courage and strength. I made it through with so many prayers and blessings. I started to learn the meaning of our existence. I realised that God created us to be kind, empathetic, compassionate human beings. He made us, so we care about people without hurting anyone. This was the new dimension of life I discovered that became the key to my success.

With two young children, I started to re-paint the canvas of my life with faith and prayers. As a first step, I decided to construct a house on the land gifted by my late father. Needless to say, it was a leap of faith to start this project, yet I took the chance. I could feel that there was God's hand at every step of my life. I remained steadfast in my prayers with pearls of patience and gratitude. As they say, where there is a will, there is a way. And that's how my house was built within two years.

I am also thankful to my parents for investing in my education. Though I no longer saw myself as a doctor, I reinvented myself. I enrolled in nutrition courses in the UK and the US. I was successfully awarded diplomas and specialisations with distinction, adding further feathers to my cap. Eventually, every hardship became a stepping stone to reach the bounties of my career as a Nutritionist.

After a long career gap, it was hard to start afresh and as a newcomer to healthcare. It was hurtful to be treated as an intern and report to junior colleagues. Nevertheless, with resilience and a positive approach, I forged ahead. "She will not die until she proves herself," became the motto for my life.

Six months of struggle as an intern gave me the courage to start my independent nutrition clinic. With determination and high ethics, I established a small health and nutrition fitness clinic, NUTRADVICE. Although I had taken the initiative, I could not afford to rent private premises to start a clinic. I desperately needed a place to start.

Consequently, I applied to various clinics to get a small space for consultations. Finally, I started providing onsite consultancy at different gyms and a small hospital as a consultant nutritionist. I also visited different clinics to consult various patients.

Sometimes I had to take my children with me and they would sit in the waiting room while I consulted patients. I had no-one to look after them, and they were too young to be home alone.

Unfortunately when you are at your weakest there are people who will try to take advantage of you. This happened to me too. As a woman trying to rebuild her life, I was considered selfish. I was being mocked, blamed for things that weren't my fault. But deep down, I knew my intentions were pure. I refused to listen to the harsh words. My aim was to provide a better life for my children who were suffering in all the chaos of a broken family home.

Hard work and patience never go unrewarded. One day, a colleague invited me to present a small segment on nutrition on national TV. I accepted eagerly. It was a great experience and opened many doors for me as a Nutritionist. I was invited to give my expert advice on nutrition by different TV and radio channels. My TV segments were such a great success that to my utter surprise and joy, I was offered a contract by a TV channel to regularly host their show as a nutritionist.

This was a great blessing that I considered as a reward for my resilience and patience. Since then, there has been no looking back. My practice started to pick up. Patients were happy with me.

When I used to walk by the hospital building where I work today, I still remember, it was under construction. I would ask my children to pray that I would get a job there once it was finished. Their innocent prayers were answered. Within six months of construction being completed I was offered the position of Head of Department of Nutrition, which I accepted with gratitude and pride.

In my heart, I have no doubt that behind every step of my achievements there were countless prayers said by my parents, siblings, family, and friends. So now my objective was to build the importance of nutrition in people's minds.

The path I chose was different from other nutritionists. I jumped into this field after completing a MBBS and MPH. Nutritionists are usually MSC and Ph.D. I was often told my skills were wasted in this field, and that being a doctor, with a specialisation in medicine, surgery, or gynaecology would be the right path. I was told so many times that the field of nutrition wouldn't lead me anywhere.

Though I was challenged at every step, I made it through. People began to recognise my face, as I was regularly doing nutrition segments on different TV channels. Nosheen, who no-one had known four years ago, is now considered one of the top nutritionists in Islamabad.

After our hardships began to ease, I started building beautiful memories with my children. I planned vacations with them to Thailand and Malaysia. I can't forget the excitement on their faces when they saw the tickets. It was priceless! My bond with my children started to get stronger and flourished. I am thankful for that.

Regardless of the difficult times in my life, I refused to accept sympathy and help from anyone. I have a strong will and a stubborn character. The Universe always has its plans. While I was in the darkest tunnel of my life, a Divine plan was in the offing, leading to a magnificent career path.

During this journey filled with ups and downs, which were emotionally, physically, and mentally draining, my family was my constant support, and were always there to hold me up in my weakest moments. Their endless support and love made me realise what I could do. I'm thankful to my family, friends and my kids without whom my journey to success was not possible.

I learnt that grief doesn't go away. Nothing heals it. You just learn to deal with grief. And when you face a difficult situation, there are two ways to go: either you surrender or you fight back.

I am glad I chose to fight back. I set an example for my children so they know the difference between right and wrong. I often hear, "Nosheen, you are so strong." Only I know how I gained this strength.

Hard work and my unrelenting desire to excel got me off to a great start both as a Nutritionist running a successful consultancy practice, and as the Head of the Nutrition Department at PAF Hospital. With time management and discipline, I found myself brilliantly raising my children and positively balancing my profession. My vision and courage moved me up the ladder. Today, my self-belief, strength, and motivation have helped me achieve milestones in my profession.

Everything happens for a reason. Have faith. My journey is not finished here. I still have a long way to go. The aim of sharing my story is to let others know, where there is a will, there is a way. You never know the ending may be the beginning of a new journey. Don't be affected by the negative labels you may be given. Listen to your heart and mind, keep your intentions clear, and don't hurt people intentionally. LOVE, LIVE AND LET LIVE.

I dedicate my journey to my late father, whom I lost to the current COVID pandemic. I am sure he is proudly watching from above.

About The Author

Dr. Nosheen Taqvi is a renowned Pakistani nutritionist and motivational speaker working as Head of Department in Nutrition in a highly reputable hospital in Islamabad. She is also CEO of the health and nutrition clinic, Nutradvice.

As a devoted and dedicated mum of two teenage kids, Dr. Nosheen has fought the negative odds in her life, and proven that if you decide to achieve something no matter what age group you belong to you can do it with hard work and perseverance.

With her aim to bring change in healthy eating and nutritional practices she has worked relentlessly to break all the myths and malpractices in nutrition.

Dr. Nosheen's inspirational journey has given hope to many women in Pakistan who are struggling to get their existence acknowledged in a traditionally male dominated society.

Dr. Nosheen can be contacted at:

Email: *nosheen.abbas1980@gmail.com*

Facebook: *https://www.facebook.com/nutradvicenosheen/*

Instagram: *https://www.instagram.com/nutradvice_by_dr_nosheen/?hl=en*

STORY ELEVEN

Into the Unknown – Living a Purpose-Driven Life

When we cautiously make suitable, relevant, genuine decisions that are true to our values, amazing things happen.

When checking the dictionary, my name, Tracy, means "*fighter*," "*bravery*"; in terms of personality, someone named Tracy is "*of high spirit and likes to make an influence on others with their energy.*" Thanks to my mother, who named me Tracy – perhaps that injected courage in me and gave my life a meaning.

Six years ago, I decided to listen to my calling. I took a leap of faith, leaving a stable corporate job and starting a business out of my passion. With an aspiration to help people succeed by maximising their strengths, demonstrating their authenticity, and communicating their stories confidently and compellingly, my "baby" – Frame & Fame – was born in November 2015. Seeing my clients succeed gives me so much satisfaction.

Believe it or not, I had never dreamt of running my own business. How did that happen? Here is a story about my transformation – in 10 Ps.

Personality & Perception

My mother gave me a lot of freedom as a child. I would make my own decisions after weighing the options. I guess that is why I got used to sailing my boat and navigating along my voyage. Such experience also nurtured my outgoing, flexible, adaptive personality. My friends and colleagues think I was born to be a communicator.

In my teenage years, I participated in many social service projects, teaming up with my peers, taking initiatives to reach out and support the disadvantaged groups in society. It was incredibly rewarding for me to know someone's lives or well-being was improved by our services.

Looking back, all these adventures provided a great learning space and laid a strong foundation in my personal and professional development. At fourteen, I had already set my eyes on a communication-related career that allowed me to work with people (instead of numbers!).

If there were a time machine, I wished I could travel back in time to advise my younger self to understand and leverage my strengths, be strategic and have foresight on career choices.

Without much planning, I simply followed a standard route and did whatever society perceived as the "right thing" to do. After graduation, I was lucky enough to be able to get into one of the largest shipping and supply chain businesses, a Fortune 500 company, as their international management trainee. I did not complete the two-year traineeship. It was one of the toughest decisions I made, but I knew I wanted to get back to a communication career from the bottom of my heart. I tried hard to keep the relationships, though. Some of the trainees have now become my good friends. Even though we are miles apart, we would still support each other in our endeavours.

In my early 20s, I cared about how others perceived me. Instead of taking charge of my own brand, I lived under other's expectations. How could I listen to someone else on what suited me best when they did not know my personality or job expectations? After spending a couple of years in the corporate world, I realised that I am at my best when I work and lead in a nimble, agile organisation with a flat structure, where I can bring my ideas to life so that I can make a positive impact to the organisation and the society directly and concretely.

Lesson learned: Following other's expectations can only get us to a place where others want us. It is important to understand our personality, our strengths, and our uniqueness. Let us care less about what others perceive as "good" and take charge of our own path, creating the desired impression that we want others to have on us.

Perfection & Procrastination

Life has no replay, rewind, nor retake options. If I could "retake," I would try my best to work on my self-doubts, controlling them from interfering with my behaviour. In my university and work life, on several occasions, I was on a good run. I was giving my best, and people were cheering for me. Suddenly, when I was approaching the finishing line, I felt I wanted to reach "utopia" (the perfect state). I instantly doubted my ability and eventually procrastinated. I withdrew, to everyone's surprise, even when everything was fine. My self-doubts had impacted both my academic and professional achievements, and my brand had been hurt repeatedly.

I must find a solution to this sabotaging behaviour.

After years of self-reflection, I acknowledged that I have always been very critical of myself. I was always the first person casting doubts about whether I could achieve what I wanted. This is likely due to my upbringing. I did not receive the approval and care that I needed as a child. Growing up, I subconsciously sought approval from others – my friends, teachers, colleagues, managers, etc. I might look confident and tough, but I was sensitive and vulnerable. I did not believe that I could succeed, and hence, I became the killer of my own achievements.

That was until seven years ago, when I hired a career coach for myself, hoping to gain a clearer vision and have breakthroughs in my career. It was one of the best decisions I have ever made! Not only the coaching process helped me clear my thoughts and be self-aware of my strengths and blind spots, but my whole vision also changed. My life transformed.

Now, I am still a "work-in-progress." Self-doubts come to my mind from time to time. After learning more about coaching, my self-awareness improved. By expressing my vulnerability, I have a much stronger mental state. Every day I remind myself not to be a perfectionist. Making progress, be it small, is far better than merely standing at the starting point, mapping out the best way in theory. I also practiced reframing my mind, "deleting" some miserable history, and owning a new narrative that I create for myself. When we cautiously make suitable, relevant, genuine decisions that are true to our values, amazing things happen.

Passion & Purpose

Very often, clients, business contacts, friends, and acquaintances asked, "What exactly is coaching? Why would you become a coach?"

Considering that there are many more coaches with various offerings globally nowadays, I would clarify that I did not set up a coaching business to do something "fancy and trendy." It is a career transition by choice, a profession that aligns my passion and a business driven by my purpose.

Coaching, in my opinion, is a continuous learning process. It is a practice. In the last decade, I have developed a niche in branding, communication, and people development. I am eager to devote my time and energy to practice coaching to help others grow and succeed.

Positivity & Perseverance

Wearing multiple hats as a coach, a consultant, and a business owner is not easy. Sometimes I see coaches and consultants who run a very commercialised business, even marketing themselves like a celebrity. Googling peers in the industry proved to be quite a toxic experience as my inferiority kicked in, and my self-doubts were waving at me. I paused and reorientated myself. As opposed to following other's paths or competing on price, programs, and qualifications, I never agree that the coaching and consulting business is purely a numbers game. It is a people business. Why not strengthen the biggest asset in my coaching and consulting business — myself and my team!

From learning and using Gallup's CliftonStrengths assessment, I mindfully put my strengths into good use and allow my teammates to play to their strengths. Altogether, we can maximise our own potentials and grow the business literally strength by strength. According to Gallup's assessment, my "Top5 Strengths" is *Woo, Communication, Positivity, Developer, and Adaptability.* Obviously, the *Communication* and *Developer* strengths are the reasons explaining why I'd naturally do well, plus I enjoy much in coaching and consulting. I apply my *Developer* and *Adaptability* in hiring, managing, and coaching my team.

In my corporate life, I seemed to have underestimated or overlooked the positive energy in me. This was especially true when I first relocated to Singapore with my then-corporate communication consultant job. I was surrounded by colleagues with a high level of negativity. No matter how much I ignored and resisted their daily moans, complaints, gossips, and negative attitude, I soon realised such negative energy had penetrated my shield and impacted my well-being. I started feeling stressed, lost, and helpless.

"You are amazingly resilient, Tracy. However, do you think you are being hurt by your own loyalty?"

A very powerful, thought-provoking question from an entrepreneur friend in Singapore. It challenged me inside out and opened my eyes to a huge blind spot. From there, I was inspired and motivated to start a new chapter in my life – stepping into the unknown. Feeling scared and excited at the same time, I took a leap of faith to quit my job and established my brand and my business, Frame & Fame.

My *Positivity* has given me the strength to be resilient in facing setbacks and getting through numerous difficulties in my entrepreneurial journey.

Running my own business does have its perks, though. Autonomy, creativity, flexibility, for instance, are definitely my thriving factors and my motivators. On this "roller coaster ride," when we can learn from experience and have better foresight on what is lying ahead, we can be prepared, and our enjoyment can be heightened.

One major learning is that when I first started my business, I would naturally compare myself with fellow entrepreneurs, especially those who run similar businesses as I do, who had a comparable structure and scale, or who started more or less the same time. I couldn't help feeling like a BIG failure and shameful whenever I discovered any of them were growing at a higher rate, getting more traction, gaining better recognition.

Juggling is no longer struggling. I can currently strive for a much better work-life balance by having a more thorough understanding of my capacity, strengths, and personal and professional goals. I am grateful that I no longer feel bad or panic when I run slower than others at times. By setting my own pace, and persevering through any challenges, I will create my success.

Public Relations & Personal Branding

Whenever I reflect on my entrepreneurial journey, I am amazed by how wonderful life can be. I used to think I got "my best deal" in the public relations industry. I was proud of my role, my team, and my company. I enjoyed my life in PR and as a communications professional. Never would I imagine a change. Never had I dreamed of having my own brand, running my own business!

"Life is like a rainbow. We need both the sun and the rain to make its colour appear."

—Zeenat

I noticed I had never been strategic in my own development. I did not pursue any long-term view of my career growth, and I took no action to create the life I envisioned myself living. I took whatever pay and position that my previous bosses gave me. I let others see me however they wanted. I counted on luck to get opportunities.

Wow, I was reactive to life events! This was a major discovery! As a positive and proactive person, why would

I not take an active role in living my life? What have I missed?

Because I was my own victim of leaving my own Personal Brand to others, which impacted so much on my income, my bargaining power, my career development, and essentially my self-worth, I want to become an advocate for personal branding. I established Frame & Fame Personal Branding and Executive Coaching.

By finding my own voice and following my life-purpose I have been able to create a business helping aspiring leaders, managers, and entrepreneurs to frame their mind, their messages, and their image so they can earn the fame (aka reputation), income, and respect they deserve.

About The Author

Tracy Ho is a leading personal branding consultant and executive presence coach. She is the Founder and Director of Frame & Fame, a personal brand consulting and executive coaching firm in Hong Kong, which was recognised as the "*Most Trusted Personal Branding Consultancy Services of the Year*" under Hong Kong Most Outstanding Business Awards for two consecutively years (2019, 2020).

Tracy believes that a clearly defined personal brand can strategically position individuals in a crowded market, enabling them to be seen, heard and known as an authentic leader, raise their share of voice in the industry, and rise to the next level. Tracy is also an experienced image consultant, international business etiquette and presentation trainer. She advises both female and male executives.

Tracy is a talented storyteller and an energising speaker. She is regularly invited to deliver keynote speeches at conferences and speak at various talks and events.

Tracy can be contacted at:

Email: *tracy@frameandfame.com*

LinkedIn: *https://www.linkedin.com/in/hotracy/*

Facebook: *https://www.facebook.com/tracyho.personalbranding*

STORY TWELVE

Journey to Purpose

I found my fulfilment in positive relationships, engaging the disengaged, recognising and supporting the vulnerable, and working to protect abused children.

I do not remember setting out on a particular path in life with certainty but have been guided by strong people, experiences, and opportunities.

I come from a small rural community in Ireland and now recognise, from a family of resilient and determined adults. I have always been inspired by the brave decision of my grandfather to educate his daughters, allowing them to become strong women who took risks and strived to reach their potential when it was not the norm to do so. My mother was the first university graduate in her family, graduating in 1947 as a specialist teacher of the hearing impaired.

Despite the promise of a rewarding career, she made the brave decision to follow her heart and crossed the Irish sea to marry my father. As a non-Gaelic speaker and unable to fulfil her life as a teacher, she began to teach children literacy skills, addressing many of the gaps in special needs provision in schools and improving the life chances of many. Not content with being a full-time mum and a part-time educator, she opened a fully inclusive early year nursery school, educating a generation of local children, working tirelessly until retirement at 73 years of age.

My father left a secure job as a white-collar worker to establish a thriving horticulture farming business. I believe that I learned my strong work ethic when we sat down for family meals. As children, we were expected to help on the farm and complete the tasks set out each day. I had the privilege of a comfortable lifestyle but was also expected to work hard. During this time, I learned about responsibility and accountability, being asked to justify decisions made during my day.

My strong will was both a blessing and a curse. I always knew best and rebelled against authority and was yet to see the value of a good education. My father's goal for me was not yet my goal. I wanted to escape the norm, to see and experience the opportunities the world had waiting for me.

Following a summer vacation in Vancouver, having completed a Childcare Certificate qualification, I seized the opportunity to follow two of my brothers and relocated to British Columbia as a nanny. During my short time in Canada, I had such fun but finally recognised that formal education was essential to secure a good standard of living and the lifestyle I wanted.

Reluctantly, I returned home, completed additional qualifications, and secured my place at Leeds Metropolitan University, 40 years after my mum's graduation. I was about to embark on the next chapter in my life. Leaving family and friends once again, I took the boat to Holyhead, Wales, to begin my new life in Leeds.

The next stage of my journey was full of the highs and lows of life. It was here that I found my sense of purpose and my tenacity. I loved teaching but recognised rather than having a love of a specialist subject. I found my fulfilment in positive relationships, engaging the disengaged, recognising and supporting the vulnerable, and working to protect abused children. I had graduated, married, and had twin girls. As a working mum, I found that resilience was much needed, but my joy in family life made it all worthwhile.

After seven years, I found myself a single mum, but I picked myself up and continued to provide the life that my girls deserved. My work ethic was strong, and my desire to be a positive role model gave me the strength to continue learning, progress, and take on new roles of responsibility.

I worked in a range of different multicultural schools and discovered the richness and rewards of diversity. As a named Child Protection Leader, I have been humbled to support too many children who shared accounts of abuse. To be the "Trusted Adult" is a privilege. The training provided for this role is often limited and can primarily focus on procedure. However, I believe that personal skills such as emotional intelligence and resilience, and a strong moral compass are equally as important to the role.

The role requires adults to go above and beyond and to become expert jugglers. My daughters understood when they were asked to "get a bowl of cornflakes for dinner" as I worked to support a vulnerable child. It is still their go-to when life is busy.

It is widely recognised that our experiences in life shape us, and many can have a positive, or sadly, a negative effect on us. One complex child protection case shaped my drive for and approach to the protection of children. I remember every detail of the child's account, the conversation with the parents and the professionals.

A fourteen-year-old child who entered my office, with a friend to offer support, confused, frightened, and scared, bravely said: "I think I am being sexually abused, but I am not sure, and I need to share my story with you." As I listened, I acted to protect, I followed the statutory requirements and process, and worked to ensure that I did the right things for the child.

However, in the weeks that followed, I took time to reflect on the case, questioning how we had found ourselves in this position at all. It raised a most important question, how can a child grow up, be educated, and not recognise abusive and harmful actions and behaviours?

We teach children a wide range of subjects and life skills in our schools, so why don't we teach children to understand and recognise harmful behaviours to understand privacy, safe touch, and consent? Many schools now deliver strong Relationship and Sexual Education Programmes; however, we must ensure that age-appropriate lessons are delivered to all children from the start of their education journey until they leave to enter the adult world.

It is not a child's responsibility to keep themselves safe but our adult responsibility to ensure that they recognise when they are unsafe and know-how and where to seek help and support. This case still drives my desire to educate to protect.

My goal was to be a Headteacher in a school and provide an environment that would meet all children's emotional, social, and academic needs. Despite my desire and drive, this was not to be my destiny, and I learned that my values and strong ethical beliefs were to force my next change in the direction of my life.

My position as a senior leader in a large secondary school became untenable when I found my professional contributions, values, beliefs, and education philosophy was not supported. This forced change rocked my professional and personal world, but I was to learn that "out of adversity comes opportunity." I loved my time as an educator and chose to continue to work within wellbeing and child protection areas in my professional life.

This next chapter of my life was born out of necessity rather than desire. However, I am eternally grateful for the enforced change. I had to dig deep, to become a risk-taker again, but mostly to overcome the "imposter syndrome" feelings I had from time to time. It was here that I reflected on my skills and personal attitudes gained along my journey to date and relied on my inner strength to guide me.

Three days after I left my school leadership role, I was on a plane to South America as part of a Specialist

Safeguarding and Child Protection Consultancy Team. I had finally found my purpose and true vocation.

My new consultancy role and 23 years in education gave me the confidence to take the leap of faith and begin sharing my learning with the International Education world. I have had opportunities to be a teacher, leader, coach, trainer, and speaker and now would use my skill set to engage others and share a vision for a "safe" school, where a "Culture of Care" would flourish.

My next appointment to a two-year administrative role in a leading international school and my move to Vietnam was made possible by the Head of School, another risk-taker. The journey of change management we took together restored my faith in courageous leadership and allowed me to trust again. Five years of life in Southeast Asia, and I learned so much. This experience was supported by many, and I made lifelong friends along the way.

I embraced the opportunity to share my vision for keeping children safe with a wider audience and to influence change. The lessons learned and successes along the way prepared me well for my role as Safeguarding Manager for Asia for a leading schools group. This role enabled me to share my philosophy on "keeping children safe" embedding an understanding of the importance of a holistic lens and a strong "Culture of Care" with a broader audience. The ripple effect of the message allowed adults to make significant differences in children's lives.

I strongly believe that life is a journey and that timing is all-important. The gravity of *feeling the fear and doing it anyway* has allowed me to embrace change and opportunities. As I reflect on my youth, I recognise the constraints of the expected. There were fleeting opportunities where I would step outside of my comfort zone, but the normality of daily life somewhat curtailed this.

My strong work ethic has been central to my success but, more importantly, allowed me to demonstrate the rewards of hard work to my children. As a family, we work together, encouraged and supported by a strong family motto, "you and me against the world". We recognise the importance of this mantra, that we are stronger together and we face and resolve issues together as a family.

I learned the importance of embracing change, even when it is unexpected or involuntary. In the two most significant life events for me, times of real adversity, I learned that whilst I could not control the actions and values of others, I could choose to grow, how to act, and respond. I aligned my values, took control and made lemonade from lemons. I made conscious decisions to let go of negative feelings and to channel my emotions positively.

During a time of significant reflection, I discovered the power of Neuro-Linguistic Programming and began to use it to change my mindset. Some of this early work set me free from deep feelings of resentment.

I deeply value friendship and recognise how essential positive relationships are to flourishing, allow room for relationships to grow and change, and recognise when a relationship has come to an end. I believe people can enter your life for a short time and make a big impact, and some are like comfort blankets, always there, quietly supportive, lifelong and offering unconditional love. Those people will always know who they are.

I believe that we grow from "paying it forward." My work as a Safeguarding and Child Protection Consultant for Fairchild Safeguarding and my various roles in leadership, coaching, mentoring and training allow me to share my learning journey in the hope that others can learn and grow too. I have learnt to listen to my inner self, reflect, identify my non-compromising values, and ensure that they remain central to my actions and decisions. I now know that *"the past is a place to be learned from, not a home to be lived in"* as stated by Robin Sharma. I invite the reader to take the time to reflect, to examine their values and beliefs, and to de-clutter their life, creating space to fill their life with meaning, people, opportunities, and experiences which fulfil them. I invite you to flourish, for you.

About The Author

Suzanne Murray is a Safeguarding, Child Protection and Wellbeing Consultant and Founder of FairChild Safeguarding Ltd. An Educator with over 30 years experience in State and International Schools, her unique skill set and unshakable belief in the value and potential of children is central to her work. Her measured and balanced approach to safeguarding turns policy into practice.

Suzanne was born and educated in Ireland and subsequently graduated from Leeds Metropolitan University with BEd Hons in Home Economics. Early in her career, she found that her desire to support children's wellbeing and safety was central to her various roles, working with and supporting vulnerable children.

Suzanne has experience of living in various countries and has developed a particular interest in culture. She advocates for the development of a "Culture of Care" in all learning organisations and uses her experience to educate, advise, train and speak to the moral duty to protect all children.

Suzanne can be contacted at:

Email: *suzanne@fcsafeguarding.com*

LinkedIn: *https://www.linkedin.com/in/suzanne-murray-fcs/*

Website: *FairChild Safeguarding | Let's make a difference (fcsafeguarding.com)*

STORY THIRTEEN

Leadership in Diaspora

When women work together as a formidable force, we break all the glass ceilings preventing women from getting to the top.

My father, Chief Dr. Josephus George Chinwah hailed from the illustrious Chinwah Dynasty of the larger Imeagi Family of Obagi Community, of Ogba/Egbema/Ndoni L.G.A. in Rivers State, Eastern part of Nigeria. And my Mother Princess Eunice Adenike Oladipo was born to the family of Late Chief Emmanuel Titus Oladipo, MFR, of Ageshinsowa Compound, Ilare Quarters, Ile-Ife and late Princess Elizabeth Ademonwo Oladipo of Olodo's Compound, Ogboru Royal Ruling House, Ilare, Ile-Ife, Osun State, Western part of Nigeria.

Born in Lagos, I am the seventh child of my mother and the tenth child of my father. I grew up in a relatively peaceful polygamous home.

I have been in leadership most of my adult life. My inspiration comes from the humility of my mother and the strength of my father's firm but loving leadership. First and foremost, I have had the opportunity to lead my family. Subsequently, I have led various women's organisations, sat on executive boards, interacted with international and government representatives, and run businesses in different parts of the world.

My husband Mr. Ibrahim James Pam's comes from a prominent family from the North Central part of Nigeria. His career as an international lawyer required that we live on four continents and we have visited over 50 countries.

My experience as an expatriate spouse has been that of exotic discovery to the ordinary and mundane. I have learned to rebrand myself to meet my immediate needs and circumstances by adapting to my new reality of being an expatriate professional outside my home country.

This global exposure has equipped me with the necessary skills and mindset needed to become a diaspora leader. As a leader in the diaspora, I need to be adaptable and flexible. This experience enables me to be a visionary and a transformative leader.

The dynamism of leading an intercontinental organisation from a remote location is an incredibly challenging experience yet a rewarding adventure at the same time. I have survived the difficulty of feeling alone and displaced from my familiar comfort zone. Having to give up my professional career, business, and educational pursuit to embark on a diplomatic journey with my husband has taken a toll on me.

What is leadership? In my research on leadership, I have found some common components in a variety of definitions. These similarities see leadership as a process that involves influence, occurs in groups, and is based on common goals. I also realised, from experience, that leadership could also be a power relationship between leaders and followers.

However, the definition of leadership that addresses leadership from the skills perspective is the most appropriate definition for my own experience as a leader in diaspora, heading and running an intercontinental organisation. My leadership style emphasises my ability, capability, knowledge, and competence to make my leadership effective. Over the many years of my career, I have acquired different administrative skills, technical skills, human skills, and conceptual skills which have prepared and enabled me to be the kind of transformational leader I am today.

What is leadership in the diaspora? It can best be defined as a cross-boundary leadership. You are operating from a remote location, not stationed in any one place, yet still have an impactful influence on your followers across international borders.

Why am I a leader in the diaspora? I am a leader who has her footprint in multiple countries and continents, not by choice but by my life circumstances. Following my husband around the world as he builds his career, I learnt to develop my career alongside him. I was determined not to be left behind in my personal, professional, and business life. It was the most significant decision of my life, and it is the key to my success and achievements in life.

As an expatriate spouse, I quickly discovered the difficulties that awaited me in pursuit of my career. I decided to do something about it and changed my circumstances. In doing so, I changed the circumstances of other expatriate spouses also disillusioned with their situations.

I founded a professional platform that could help me and other women in a similar situation integrate productively into our new countries and keep our curriculum vitae active so that we could compete favourably with our peers when we returned home from our diplomatic service.

The creation of my network, the Expat Professional and Business Women's Network (EPBWN) International in Tunisia 2013 catapulted me into the global stage and turned me into a Diaspora Leader.

As a diaspora leader, I add value to both the countries I live in and my home country. I am uniquely positioned to bridge the gap and connect many fragmented but common ideas scattered across continents. I have developed a cross-boundary leadership style due to my diplomatic lifestyle.

I specialise in leading my organisation beyond cultural, religious, and political principles. I have been able to impact lives across continents, amplify the efforts to fight global issues on my platform, connecting a community of people who support, challenge, and collaborate to create waves of change and a common purpose in our global society.

So, what is my experience? As a leader in the diaspora, I have been involved in advocacy against gender-based violence, capacity building, mentoring, coaching and empowerment of women over three decades, and have grasped these roles professionally and ethically. This has resulted in changing the lives of vulnerable women for the better.

I developed an aptitude for inspiring my teams across countries and continents. To meet the needs of my followers who are from different cultures, religious beliefs, economic and political backgrounds, I had to reset my mindset, see people, respect them, and hear people from their core values. This enabled me to have the appropriate impact on their lives or circumstances.

Over the years my leadership has evolved to a level where my conveying power, my ability to lead, hold and unite people together for a common cause have improved and grown internationally. I am comfortable and confident in my ability to achieve my set goals within any country or political framework I find myself in.

I believe that leadership can only be successful if there are good followers, who believe in my vision and accept me as their leader. Without such acceptance from my followers, leadership becomes a burden for me as a leader in a diaspora.

To me, leadership means the ability or capacity to deliver on the peoples' trust in my vision for change or progress in a family, society, or organisation. I have also found that leadership styles change in different environments. One individual can have multiple leadership styles to portray their culture or circumstances. I also appreciate that leadership can be formal and informal. It is the leader who decides on the appropriate leadership style.

These definitions of leadership resonate with me because having lived a nomadic diplomatic lifestyle over the past two decades, founding and consequently leading an international organisation has not been easy. Accordingly, I have acquired and learnt how to blend with my community to succeed or deliver my mandate as a diaspora leader.

The plight of the expatriate spouse has not been paid enough attention. We have been mistaken to be a group of leisured and comfortable women travelling the world and so what would be our problem?

Our experience is that international and diplomatic organisations do not adequately address our needs. We are treated as dependents instead of a well-educated, resourceful group of professionals who have chosen their families over their careers to advance the careers of their working spouses. Imagine the economic boom for international civil service and diplomatic institutions, if countries will intentionally tap into the professional and business acumen of expatriate spouses and provide or create opportunities for them to contribute to their host countries' economic development.

It is my desire as a diaspora leader to empower accompanying expatriate spouses and vulnerable women to achieve financial independence and professional success, build their confidence, and help create leadership capacity in them. My greatest passion as a diaspora leader is creating mentoring opportunities, developing, and starting up businesses and job placements for my followers in their professional development in their various countries as accompanying spouses. This huge mandate has challenged my leadership and has taught me how to be a better leader for upcoming expatriate spouses struggling to discover themselves.

EPBWN International provides a platform for developing and promoting educational and training programs geared towards advancing women's professional and personal lives. It empowers women by sharing their experiences, skills, and knowledge to promote the well-being of women.

My challenges as a leader in Diaspora!

The fundamental challenge to my leadership in the diaspora is my adaptive leadership style which also created adaptive challenges for me. These challenges are not easily identified, not straightforward kinds of problems. And the solution is not reliant on me alone but on many factors that give a bigger picture of the whole situation.

As a diaspora leader, I need the support and understanding of my followers across the board to succeed. This creates an obstacle, as this involves changing people's mindsets, behaviours, priorities, beliefs, and values. Having to often deal with complex situations across different countries requires that I step back from my own struggles and look for the proper perspective in this challenging situation.

When I step away from all the noise, chaos, and activities,

I am able to see the larger picture and clearly identify what is happening without being biased. My greatest challenge has always been how can I change the mindset of my followers without exposing them to the vulnerability that comes with the changing concept?

I have come to appreciate the power of language, first as a Linguist then as a leader in the diaspora. Language is a powerful tool for any nation or people's economic, political, and social development. As a diaspora leader, I need to utilise language to expand the EPBWN International. Introducing the local language alongside English to reach our targeted audience has automatically encouraged every calibre of women to join EPBWN International.

However, I would say I have been privileged to be in positions of leadership across continents. And I have enjoyed every bit of it. I also acknowledge the growth and exposure this has afforded me as an innovative and ethical leader on an international stage. My desire would be to leave a legacy of a leader in the diaspora who gave equal opportunity to all women, who impacted her community, who empowered various women and opened the opportunities for them to be financially independent. I want to be remembered for leaving a trace of myself in every city, town, and country I have lived.

In conclusion, my call to action for you, the reader, is that every human being must have an attitude of planning, envisioning, organising, and controlling the circumstances surrounding their lives. Take charge of the direction, synthesise, focus on relevant issues, coordinate, educate, and develop yourself at every opportunity.

This attitude will propel you far in life because you will not leave anything to chance. Always have a bigger picture in mind as you execute your duties as a leader.

The power of collaboration is immense. Never stand alone. Networking and forming alliances is the greatest tool available for anyone who wants to be a visionary and transformational leader. Model ethical and moral practices by being fair-minded, dependable, and standardising leadership across boundaries.

I want to end with these words: always seek information concerning anything you want to achieve; do not go along with what other people are saying. Go to the source to get the appropriate information. That way, you cannot be misled and miss opportunities.

Seek excellence in all you do in a firm, loving and caring manner where it builds your followers without destroying their self-esteem or discouraging them from aspiring.

Above all, when women work together as a formidable force, we break all the glass ceilings preventing women from getting to the top.

About The Author

Princess Nwakego Ibrahim-Pam is a seasoned expatriate spouse, an educationist, linguist, inspirational speaker, transformational leader, social entrepreneur, mentor, philanthropist, employer, trainer, and administrator.

She is the Founder and Chairperson of the Expat Professional and Business Women's Network International. She is also the Founder and Executive Director of Petra Speech and Early Childhood Developmental Centre, Co-Founder of the Korea Africa Economic Association, and Co-Founder of the Spousal Association of the Green Climate Fund.

Princess Nwakego worked with the International Criminal Court (ICC) in The Hague, at the International Criminal Tribunal for the former Yugoslavia in The Hague, and with the British Council in Nigeria. She is a member of the Ifez Community Consultative Committee. She received the Medal of Honour from the Nigerian Government and also received an Award of Appreciation from the IFEZ

Authority. She is a member of the International Society of Female Professionals (ISFP).

Princess Nwakego Ibrahim-Pam can be contacted at:

Email: *Info.epbwnsk@gmail.com*

LinkedIn: *https://www.linkedin.com/in/princess-nwakego-aka-kego-ibrahim-pam-01201414/*

Website: *https://epbwnt.weebly.com/*

STORY FOURTEEN

Listen to Your Inner Voice

Ask yourself what you are deeply yearning for? When the answers flow, you will see that they are based in aligning yourself with your own personal integrity and what that means to you.

It's August 1999, and I'm standing at Heathrow Airport, with conflicting emotions, feeling utterly heartbroken and yet excited. As I walk through immigration, I take off my engagement ring because I know in my heart of hearts that even though I still love the man I thought I was going to marry, the relationship will not fulfil me.

I was on my way to Hong Kong to take up the role of Head of Food and Nutrition at an international school. Initially, I had planned for my fiancé to join me, but as the time grew nearer, I knew this would never happen, and so I arrived in this vibrant new city alone.

There was, however, no time to dwell on my emotions. The sounds and the smells of the city were overwhelming. The fast pace, the red taxis, the Chinese calligraphy, and the wonderful noodle shops all fascinated me.

The resources at my new school were fabulous, and the children were a joy to teach. I threw myself into work with enthusiasm. However, once I'd settled in, I realised that I still had unanswered questions about my former relationship and my difficult yet strong decision to be alone. I knew I wanted to dig deep, understand myself better, and learn how to make better choices.

As I was mulling these thoughts over, I came across a book by Rhonda Britten called "Fearless Loving." I was immediately drawn to it and read it in a single sitting.

It was after reading this book that I knew I wanted to become a coach.

I can't remember a time when I didn't want to help people, so it's no surprise that I'm now a health coach with a functional medicine approach. Even at a very early age, I can remember packing a little satchel with first aid equipment and setting off to look for people to heal. My mum was a nurse, so she was obviously my role model in this respect.

I always trust my gut instincts, and when in doubt, I pray and meditate, and the answers always come to me. I feel as though I have an inner guiding light. Looking back, I can clearly see how I was destined to work as a health coach, even though I started studying Home Economics, Food Science, and Nutrition.

I began training to be a Certified Fearless Living Coach. I gained levels one and two and went on to study with Tony Robbins completing Mastery University by getting out of my comfort zone, jumping off telegraph poles and breaking wooden boards with my bare hands.

I was taught by my parents that "anything is possible" and Tony Robbins' Mastery University course reinforced this belief. I have always lived in the belief that we create our own reality with our thoughts, and denying this takes away our power.

Through the courses I studied, I learned so much that helped me overcome the emotional crisis I'd been through when I broke off my engagement, and I wanted to help others in similar situations. This was my motivation for starting my first coaching practice, which I ran alongside my work at the school.

It was soon after this that my passion for travel led to another life-changing moment. I was on holiday in Cambodia when I came across a small child one evening as I was strolling back to my accommodation. He couldn't have been more than three years old. He was squatting in the gutter, wearing nothing but filthy underpants, whimpering in distress. I stopped and looked around and quickly realised there were no adults anywhere. The boy was all alone. When I tried to communicate with him, he recoiled and seemed afraid. He clearly couldn't understand. I waited and waited, but nobody came, and I realised that there was nothing I could do to help this tiny, abandoned child.

Back at my hotel that night, I found it impossible to sleep. As I lay in bed, a burning desire to help orphans and homeless people in Cambodia was ignited.

On my return to Hong Kong, I spent my first morning crying for a very long time. I was deeply saddened by the things I'd witnessed in Cambodia, and donating money simply was not enough for me anymore. On Monday morning, I set about making enquiries, and the right contacts in Cambodia began to show up as if by magic. A picture emerged of how I could take a team of students from my school to build houses for the homeless in Cambodia.

When I stopped to think about what I was doing, I felt overwhelmed. This challenge took me further out of my comfort zone than I had ever been. Yet, my Fearless Living Coach training helped me overcome my fears, and I pioneered a community service project called "Caring for Cambodia." Over the course of the next decade, I took 488 students from Hong Kong to Cambodia, where we built 180 houses and raised over US$320,000.

Along the way, I helped many orphaned and HIV-positive children in Cambodia. The project also had a profound effect on the Hong Kong students who took part. Witnessing the poverty in Cambodia, they told me how grateful they were for the comforts of their own lives and the love of their parents.

As for myself, I gained confidence in my leadership skills, and I learned a valuable lesson – that leadership is about action and not position.

For the following few years, I continued to teach and coach until one day, out of the blue, I began to suffer from heart palpitations. It was an alarming experience. My heart was racing for no obvious reason, and I felt very unwell. I found somewhere to sit down, convinced that I was suffering a heart attack. After a few minutes, the palpitations stopped, but I felt shocked by the experience and started searching for a medical explanation.

My doctor recommended wearing a heart monitor for twenty-four hours, and I discovered I was suffering from heart arrhythmia and that my heart was skipping beats. As if this wasn't frightening enough, I also suffered from memory loss. I struggled to remember my students' names, and I even forgot the name of someone I'd known for over thirteen years. I knew something was wrong with my health.

At first, my symptoms were a mystery to my doctor. My health was deteriorating, but nobody could tell me what was wrong. Spending hours scouring the internet and reading medical books, I tried to figure out what was causing these problems. I was so tired all the time, and yet I struggled to sleep at night. My brain fog increased, and I developed eczema on my hands and feet.

I couldn't figure out what was going wrong, and yet intuitively, I felt it was a hormonal imbalance. My search led me to an ebook by Dr. Mark Hyman, which I discovered during my training as a Health Coach with the Institute for Integrated Nutrition. Suddenly, I knew I had found the answer, and I asked my doctor for the appropriate tests. When I received the results, the answer was clear. I had Hashimoto's Thyroiditis. I was put on medication, which immediately helped.

My passion for nutrition continued, and I used my knowledge to heal myself. Over time, I managed to get one of my thyroid antibodies back into normal range by following a strict diet and taking the right supplements. It still mystified me why I had developed this disease when I'd always eaten well and looked after myself. I continued with my health research and discovered that one of the underlying causes of Hashimoto's is SIBO or Small Intestinal Bacterial Overgrowth. A condition often confused for IBS (Irritable Bowel Syndrome) can cause gastritis, gas, and bloating.

Compromised gut health usually causes SIBO. I had suffered some severe cases of food poisoning in SE Asia and had taken many courses of antibiotics as a child because of recurrent tonsillitis, so my gut health was in a poor state.

It was this health crisis which ultimately led to a change of direction in my life. I discovered Functional Medicine and enrolled with the School of Applied Functional Medicine. I began the course with so much enthusiasm, but my health challenges continued. Just a few months into my course, I was diagnosed with Carpal Tunnel Syndrome in my right hand, and an operation was scheduled.

I was still working to heal my gut and thyroid issues, and this third health challenge was yet another setback. Two weeks after the operation on my right hand, I was told I would need the same surgery on my left hand. I believe it was Divine intervention that the surgeon did not show up when I attended my next appointment. She was stuck in the operating theatre with another patient who needed her more than I did at that moment.

After everything I had already been suffering, I couldn't face another operation. I asked for guidance in a quick prayer, and I immediately heard my inner voice saying, "Right, that's it, there has got to be another solution. Go home and find it!"

It was the word "solution" that came through loud and clear, so as soon as I arrived home, I Googled "carpal tunnel solution" and came across a website where I found a non-surgical answer, a hand orthosis that creates stretching therapy to restore flexibility to the soft tissue around the narrow passage. I ordered the product, it worked, I never had the second operation, and I've never had a problem since.

The more I questioned traditional western medical treatments, the more I realised that there are alternative healing solutions. My prayers had been answered, and my guiding light was leading me, not only towards better health but also towards a new career.

I drew my inspiration from my father, who started his own business when I was ten years old. As I was growing up, I watched his hard work and determination to succeed, and I knew I wanted to be fully self-employed in my health coaching practice by age fifty-five.

Looking back, my career has been through three separate phases. The restaurant manager, the teacher, and finally the health and wellness entrepreneur.

Reflecting on my life's journey, I can see that there have been challenges along the way, yet each of these has led me towards further growth. My first was a relationship crisis which led me on a quest to find my own strong voice in the world, to have clarity around my decision making and to set firm boundaries with myself and others. This led me to the inspirational world of Fearless Living. The second was a health crisis that led me to discover Functional Medicine and fulfil the ambition I'd had since I was a child when I packed my satchel with a first aid kit and set off to heal people.

In closing, I'd like to invite you to imagine your own death and that you are writing your own eulogy. What would you like it to say? I did this exercise in my early forties, and it was profound.

Whilst we have no idea when we're going to die, the likelihood is that after doing this, you too will realise the value of every minute you have and how you should make the most of it. Ask yourself what you are deeply yearning for?

When the answers flow, you will see that they are based in aligning yourself with your own personal integrity and what that means to you. We all yearn for a life filled with love, joy, freedom, and peace, and it is in finding our own way to fully express ourselves as unique human beings that deep happiness resides. Believe that anything is possible, listen to your inner voice, and never give up on your dreams.

About The Author

Helen Revans is the Founder of Nurture Your Life and a Certified Health Coach specialising in gut health. Helen has 30 years' experience as a Food Preparation and Nutrition educator.

Originally from Wallasey, Merseyside in the UK and now based in Hong Kong, Helen holds a BSc in Home Economics majoring in Nutrition. She was Hong Kong's first Fearless Living Life Coach.

Helen has designed a range of workshops including topics such as: "How to Address Malnutrition" in Palawan, Philippines. Helen is currently studying with The School of Applied Functional Medicine and brings a functional medicine approach to her coaching.

Helen has led service projects to Cambodia where she built and funded 180 houses. She is passionate about educating, empowering and inspiring people to live healthier, happier lives, one person, one meal and one step at a time.

Helen can be contacted at:

Email: *helen@nurtureyourlife.com*

Website: *www.nurtureyourlife.com*

Facebook: *https://www.facebook.com/nurtureyourlifewellness*

STORY FIFTEEN

Mind : A Beautiful Servant & A Dangerous Master

We have 25,000 - 70,000 thoughts a day and around 85% of our thoughts are negative and around 95% are repetitive. The power of the mind and the thoughts we have are the leading cause to who we are at any given time in our life.

Imagine a city girl who grew up with all the confidence and support that is needed for her to be a fine woman, losing her voice. This is a story of me finding my voice, amidst all the voices growing inside my mind.

I grew up in a close-knit family in Mumbai, India. My weekends were spent around many cousins, and their parents. You could experience all the human emotions under one roof in our huge family room.

Unlike my older cousins, my generation was liberated, in that we were given the opportunity to speak our minds respectfully. The demeanour of my views would depend on the side that I picked.

As you could imagine, the dynamics of that room were difficult. It changed with time, people and influences. I started off picking the safe and agreeable side, leading me to gradually lose *my voice.*

The voices in my head weren't my own, they belonged to the most influential people in that room. Most of the time I was under pressure, felt vulnerable and was searching for my belonging. Now when I look deeper, I feel empty about myself, that I traded my self-worth for belonging.

After a few setbacks in my thirties, I looked deeper into my hardwired mind and combobulated the misery that my mind had crafted for me. It brought back memories of growing up and my value system. I've been told over the years that if I do good, good will happen to me.

I love stories and the beautiful art of storytelling, and our mind is our best and the worst storyteller. Growing up I was enchanted by the stories of lord *Rama* and *Krishna*. Now, I wanted to fathom the real meaning behind those stories.

The Bhagavad Gita is popularly known to answer all the questions of being in eighteen yogas. The lessons I learned about controlling the mind, lie in just two words: *Vairagya* and *Abhyasa*. Together in Sanskrit they mean "to practise."

Separately *Vairagya* means "to detach" and *Abhyasa* means "to study." Growing up in a society that holds values that are clearly defined as black and white, and wrong or right – *Devā* and *Danavā* (gods and demons), I rarely had the opportunity to look at various shades in between.

When I brought *Vairagya* and *Abhyasa* masteries into my life, I developed a strong will to control my mind. These ideologies led me to look further into various ancient practices.

I connected with the popular Japanese samurai technique of *Fudoshin* – "an immovable mind." Imagine you are abstaining from eating sweets, and at a party all you can eat are sweets. This is that space where the mind will push you and tell stories that will change your decision. *Fudoshin* trains us to harness our energy to be firm and remain true to our promises.

These are some practises that can change the inner climate of mind, however it is easier said than done. In keeping with my social values, there were elements of dehumanisation. While growing up my mind was hardwired to dehumanise, or in simple terms to pick sides. That led to an ongoing story in my mind; constantly judging and adding angles. It would take me from a beautiful enchanted forest to the deepest dungeon, in a fraction of a second.

My mind was channelled to look around for both good and bad, my hardwired mind chose to pick sides where "bad" dwelled. It built a castle of stories and sequences of how when the opportunity presented itself, I would take the baton in my hand to lecture the lessons of moral behaviour to the bad. Stories that kept my mind occupied, normally never occurred and the opportunity for such theatrics is unreal.

Perish the thought, if one day this does occur, I have the scenarios that my mind created, well-rehearsed to give a moral lecture to the presumed "*bad.*" Wait, stop! Why am I doing this to myself? Who am I to take this responsibility to teach moral lessons? Who gives me the authority?

I needed to look further, deeper and find the purpose of my being. I don't need to have this constant story with various plots, and sides to take away the beautiful space in my mind that is honing false rehearsals. My mind needs to be curious, creative and focused on learning, loving and being kind.

From the time we arrive in this world, the discovery of self is the constant evolution, research suggests we have 25,000 - 70,000 thoughts a day and around 85% of our thoughts are negative and around 95% are repetitive. The power of the mind and the thoughts we have are the leading cause to who we are at any given time in our life. Largely, we all have old stories and self-limiting beliefs playing on repeat. I conjured my external surroundings and started to internalise each thought and absorb the reactions.

I had thousands of frustrated and negative thoughts often related to perfectionism, slow achievement and so on. I had a firm belief that success is the measure of happiness. It was a lengthy phase of my life, where I was living and loving based on other's opinions and judgements, yet I was never content. I was falling for external beauty, and joined the herd. It affected my self-confidence, authenticity, accepting *imperfections* and my ability to share love and receive love.

We must know our thought-culture. For me the strength of my body, the strength of my mind, my success and the pleasures I bring to others by my company – all depend on the nature and the quality of my thoughts.

In recent years there have been many books written on how to harness the power of the mind, each thought it cultivates, defines our success and the path that we wish to lead in our life.

Well I don't think we have cracked that recipe as yet, it is still a work in progress for us and we have merely scratched the surface. There is a lot to explore. Even so we cannot deny:

- Our thoughts heal us.
- Our thoughts have power to bring clarity in our life.
- Our thoughts are our character builders.
- Our thoughts weave our destiny.
- Our thoughts are necessary for our being.

Many great theories have been written about the thoughts that control our mind and how we are subject to them. Let me share some easy and simple practises of *Vairagya*, *Abhyasa,* and *Fudoshin* that over time have helped me master my thoughts.

We all have that one moment in the day that makes us truly happy. It can be caused by people or nature in general. This is our good thought moment and we wish to prolong it. In active practise we decide to use our mind to build castles of related thoughts.

For example, I received a surprise parcel of cookies. The taste instantly takes me back to my childhood when my mum baked those cookies. This is the moment of delight and my mind is emitting positive signals, and if this emotion has a colour then I believe it should be a nice yellowish pink – a love pastel.

Now my mind has led me to a party that I recently attended with my childhood friends where they all spoke about my mum's cookies. At that party a good friend wore an attractive dress and shared stories about our childhood – the colours of my thoughts are still in love pastel.

Then another friend brought up the topic of childhood fights and arguments. Swiftly the colours of my thoughts were getting darker. The chain of thoughts made my day gloomy.

Thoughts are our own real children. We have to be careful of our thought progeny. An evil thought will bring misery and trouble. Just as we rear our children with great care, we also have to rear good, sublime thoughts with great care.

What if I told you that we can turn our thoughts around, we can be INTENTIONAL about sequencing our thoughts to prolong the feeling of good. The moment we realise that the mind is beginning to play with us, we can SWITCH and lead it to another good thought, memory or a task. The job is not done yet, as we know we are trying to be intentional about prolonging the thoughts and feelings, our clever mind knows it too. It is a stern fighter and will try its best to win over our intentions.

Instead of fighting back, we have to show some kindness and strike a conversation with our mind, and repeat the affirmation, "It's ok if you decide to be steady today, I am kind to you and I will not fight back". Then we try once again until it becomes our best friend, bringing *Fudoshin*, *Abhyasa*, and *Vairagya* into practise.

Moving forward it is not sufficient that our thoughts are not bad. We must transmute bad thoughts into good thoughts. We ought to make them helpful thoughts. When they are sent out, they must be capable of doing immense good and benefit to the suffering of humanity and our neighbours. A good thought has the power to influence our environment.

With practise we can take full control of ourselves, the buttons of self-belief, trust and happiness are right under our palms. We can become the master to activate these energies naturally and with honesty.

We often hear affirmations like, "I love myself and I am enough." A part of loving ourselves is to be kind to ourselves, be kind to our mind. Let our mind love us and we can reciprocate with kindness.

With this practice we make conscious choices to experience joy, love and be in a state of happiness. The days when we are feeling the negative rush of the blood in our minds for various reasons, are the moments we should choose to be kind to our mind and let those emotions pass without resistance.

Once we master this art with *Fudoshin*, *Abhyasa*, and *Vairagya* we tune our memories to form a chain of experiences and thoughts that will support our growth, improve our ability to absorb information and treat every individual equally. This in turn drives us towards humanity, elevates us to be the best version of ourselves mentally and socially – without judgements.

Let's exercise this together.

Think about a memory that generates any of these emotions:

- Anger
- Hate
- Sadness
- Disgust

Now that it is in your memory, I assume it cannot be changed, because you have a feeling associated with this incident. What if I tell you that you have the power to change the past? We can all change our past, because our past is our memory and a story associated with that particular incident. Remember we are the master of our own story and our memories are the stories we tell ourselves. We can change our past by changing its narrative and the story we tell ourselves for the years to come. This will help us redefine our values and make strong connections within ourselves.

Our measure of living life to fullest is not the dollars that we saved in our bank accounts. Our measure is to maximise life experiences and living and learning each day. Train our mind to be curious, focus on the information that is required for creation and innovation – that is how humanity thrives. These are the pillars of a balanced mind.

About The Author

Sheetal Ganeriwal is a successful brand marketing professional with over 10 years of experience in various marketing roles in Asia. As a marketer, she is a lifelong storyteller, and passionate about crafting authentic brand stories. She believes our mind is a castle of fantasies. Our life experiences are excerpts of our daily conversations with our mind.

Sheetal loves to research ancient practices and stoics from around the world. When she is not speaking or crafting stories, she loves her workout, writing, kayaking and laughing till her face hurts.

Sheetal can be contacted at:

Email: *ganeriwal.sheetal@gmail.com*

LinkedIn: *https://www.linkedin.com/in/sheetalganeriwal/*

Instagram: *https://www.instagram.com/sheismespeaks/*

STORY SIXTEEN

Organized Insanity

From failures, I learnt resilience. From exclusion, I learnt to be inclusive and be a mentor to all. From not being heard, I found my voice. And at every step, I found "people" who taught me, challenged me, and forced me to become a better version of myself.

For as long as I can remember, I have been passionate about people: hearing their stories; revelling in their positivity; connecting with them at a deeper level. When I grew up, this turned into a passion for travelling the world, eating at local haunts, exploring cultural nuances, and figuring out what makes people who they are.

I never realised that these innocent encounters would one day catapult my life into the global orbit and allow me to write my success story, both as a professional and a human being.

The Caterpillar

As a child, my biggest joy was taking long walks with my dad. My dad was different from most fathers from a small-town in India of the 1970s. He was superbly calm, an ocean of wisdom, a passionate consumer of knowledge, highly empathetic, and one with a sense of justice that is hard to replicate. He refused to bring me up as his Little Girl; instead, he raised me to be a "thoughtful soldier," observant of everyone and unafraid to speak my mind.

That meant growing up, my life was far from easy. Looking back, I can see that my dad, in his quiet and firm way, forced me to put people first, think beyond myself, take on the most controversial topics, and have the self-assurance to chart my own path.

A Road Unpaved

I have spent most of my adult life in the public eye. From building Access Alts Asia as the first investment bridge between East and West to being awarded the Woman of Influence Award 2020 by the American Chamber of Commerce, my every move has been watched by the investment community globally. But also watching it are countless young women aspiring to succeed in the highly competitive and male-dominated world.

Growing up, I always knew I was different. I wanted to band with smart minds, and I wanted to create communities, though it was not seen as a real career then.

Advocating for my career path in the early 1990s, I realised a few things about myself: I was good at spotting trends early and smelling opportunities. I was ambitious and unabashed about it. I was not afraid to take risks.

After cutting my teeth in India, I moved to Hong Kong in my early 20s and set up my family office to invest in Asia that was transforming at a rapid pace. From being the sleepy backwater, Asia was becoming the growth engine of the world, home to three billion of the world's population whose lives were changing due to wealth creation, digitalisation, and economic progress.

A Passion for People

While I had no formal training as an investor, my deep love for people and understanding of their psychology served as the cornerstone for my family office investments. I picked businesses that did well for people. I backed concepts that changed the lives of people. And I picked investment partners that were people of great integrity, courage, and humility.

My journey as an investor earned me street credits and laurels as the first female Chief Investment Officer of a family office in the region. But it also set the foundation for the establishment of my investment platform, Access Alts Asia.

The Power of Network

In 2015, the opportunity knocked again. I sensed the acute need for a platform that created a network of global investors and innovators that brought strategic capital and technology to Asia. The challenge was that Asia was seen as an outpost – an opaque market that was hard to access by the Western world.

It was then that I decided to set up Access Alts Asia to bridge this gap, and in the process switched gears from being an investor to an entrepreneur. Once again, people were at the heart of it. I had built a wonderful network of global investors over 25 years, swapping intelligence and building trust with them, and it was time to leverage on that.

Started as a simple idea-sharing platform in Hong Kong, Access Alts experienced exponential growth into an influential global investment club, channelling smart capital into transformative companies. The club created the concept of discreet, intimate Member Meets in global centers such as New York, Dubai, London, Washington, San Francisco, Hong Kong, and Shanghai.

I had inadvertently pioneered the first global bridge between Asia and the rest of the world, and in the most unconventional way. I had found a way to create an interconnected community of remarkable people from all around the world who are passionate about making a difference and protecting our future.

In 2019, I was invited by Warren Buffet to take a delegation to the annual Berkshire Hathaway AGM, seen as the Mecca of the investment world. The same year, several Middle East governments invited us for potential global cooperation. And in 2020, The Milken Institute invited me to lead a discussion on Asia and Women Empowerment.

But as Covid hit, Access Alts was hit harder. Generations-old businesses were decimated, and the investment landscape changed overnight. We had to adapt quickly, turning the club into a 360 degree business consultancy.

Tears and Failures

The world now sees me as a strong, positive, and confident professional. But to become that, I had to transform myself as a person.

I got married very young and sadly never enjoyed the acceptance from my marital family. While being educated and progressive in many ways, the family found my independence of thought and action difficult to comprehend, resulting in hilarious (and often hurtful) encounters.

My moment of reckoning came one winter morning when I returned from a Bloomberg interview that highlighted my work, to find my family members complaining about a chipped teacup. I walked over to the mirror that day and promised myself that I would no longer pretend to be someone I am not.

It was at that moment that I felt unshackled. It was at that moment that I found the desire to be unapologetically myself. And it was at that moment that I gave my ambition a free ride. I felt my spirits soaring. I decided that I wanted "everything" and saw the road to a global empire - clear and shining.

Every Trough Ends In A Crest

Over the years, I have come to see my journey with my marital family as an integral part of my self-growth.

In trying to please my new family, I learnt invaluable skills. In trying to imitate them, I learnt to be elegant. In trying to advocate for myself, I learnt to speak up.

Again, when I began working in a male-dominated world of investing, I faced similar challenges. I had to work hard to earn my stripes, I had to prove myself to shatter every glass ceiling, and I had to win the respect of everyone around me. There were numerous times I failed. But each time, I dusted myself, got up, and was never shy to try again.

From failures, I learnt resilience. From exclusion, I learnt to be inclusive and be a mentor to all. From not being heard, I found my voice. And at every step, I found "people" who taught me, challenged me, and forced me to become a better version of myself.

Impact In Our DNA

People marvel at my commercial success, but I strongly believe that the Impact DNA, so deeply rooted in my mindset, is responsible for that. This stems from my Baba (my paternal grandfather), who had great privilege coming from a family of influential landowners in pre-independence India. But instead of languishing in his privilege, he dedicated his life to uplifting the people in the 200 or so villages his family-owned.

You see, my Baba once had an epiphany that despite all his riches, he could only eat three meals a day.

From that day on, he decided that everything else he had was to do with others and spent his life building schools, critical surgery hospitals, and Ashrams to help the people. He fought against social evils such as dowry and married his seven sons without any dowry, thus setting an example in the land.

My Baba died when I was very young, but his simple philosophy remained deeply ingrained in me: Excellence in Everything and Simplicity of Living.

With great privilege comes great responsibility, and I truly believe that creating Impact is our way of shouldering that responsibility.

Have Your Cake and Eat It Too

Some folks have 100% energy. I have 110%. A true Arian, I believe in getting into things headfirst. I have a zillion ideas bubbling into my head at the same time, and I want to execute them all. Conventional wisdom says that women should be content with less. I say we should want it all. I want to be a fabulous mom, I want to cultivate a beautiful garden, I want to serve on charity boards, I want to be an inspiration, and I want to have weekly cocktails with my friends, in addition to running a global business. As I reach my 50th birthday milestone, I want to be super fit, I want to delve into new business ideas, and I want to pick up golf.

To all the women reading this, I want to say that don't hold yourself back. As women, we have a genetic memory of multi-tasking. Try asking the men in your lives to get kids ready for school, hit the gym, kick ass at work, charm your way with the nanny, ace PTAs, fix dinner and still be able to slip into a cocktail dress with red lipstick – and they would be in tears!

But we as women do this every day, effortlessly. So, realise your true power and build a tribe of strong, successful women around you that become your partners-in-crime.

Paying It Forward

My passion for people also excites me about Move4Migrants and ModernMigrants, two aid organisations run by my kids to empower the migrant and minority communities of Hong Kong.

In many ways, I feel like my biggest accomplishment are my kids, who are as empathetic as they are pragmatic, who are as confident as they are humble, and who truly want to create a better world, whether through social equality or clean energy or just through inclusiveness. Looking at them, I feel it is a job well done, and I feel my values and my work will live on in them long after I am gone.

The Best is Yet To Come

As I enter the last year of my 40s, I cannot help but reflect on how blessed I feel. I am the fittest that I have ever been, and I am putting in my best work ever. I am creating the most "Change" that I can, and I am the closest to my kids (in our own topsy-turvy way) ever.

I am so much at ease with myself. All the insecurities of the early years are fading away, and I am revelling in the confidence of being a woman, being a brown woman, being a working mom, and having an excellent life-partnership with my husband.

My journey, of course, remains incomplete. I also know that I have often been less than perfect, I have had to give up relationships that were toxic, and I have had to create my own global family that supports my crazy self, GETS me, and holds me up when I fall. Will age bring perfection? Probably not. But it can bring acceptance.

I feel excited about what my 50s will bring. I dream of 20 pounds more, I dream of travelling the world, and I dream of discovering new and amazing things with my global tribe of equally crazy friends.

It's a good day. I love my life, and yes, my journey remains Unfinished!

About The Author

Aradhna Dayal is the founder and CEO of Access Alts Asia, a Hong Kong-based investment club that aims to bring global investors and technology to Asia. She also manages her family office investing in real estate, technology and healthcare.

Aradhna was the first female Chief Investment Officer in Asia, setting up her family office in Hong Kong 25 years ago. A power networker, she pioneered the "Asia-Global Summit."

She is passionate about women's empowerment and building a diverse inclusive society. She chairs Women on Boards, a powerful network of women leaders from around the world to mentor female talent in boardrooms.

In 2020 Aradhna was invited by The Milken Institute and former US Secretary of State, Madeleine Albright, to lead a discussion on mentoring Future Women Leaders in Abu Dhabi.

In recognition of her work, Aradhna was awarded the American Chamber of Commerce "Women of Influence" Award.

Aradhna can be contacted at:

Email: *CEO@accessalts.com*

LinkedIn: *https://www.linkedin.com/in/aradhna-dayal-590a8037/*

Website: *https://www.accessalts.com/*

STORY SEVENTEEN

Serenity Amidst Chaos

Another opportunity knocked on my door.
As, I have always believed in the power of Karma.
Do your bit, and things will come around.

Hailing from a small town in the southern part of India, Visakhapatnam (popularly known as Vizag), I was never exposed to the outside world and was brought up in a highly watchful and protective environment. However, my mom, who has been my pillar of strength, always wanted me to be a strong and financially independent woman.

In June 1996, after completing my MBA, I went to Mumbai – the city of dreams – to attend my cousin's wedding. Mumbai is a city that never sleeps and is known for making or breaking lives. I was stepping into India's financial hub for the very first time. Upon arrival, the pace and energy of the city instantly drew me in.

I made up my mind that this was an opportunity I couldn't afford to miss. I quickly set out to look for a job. I contacted some friends, and they helped connect me with a few companies. I got my first interview with a software company selling anti-virus software.

I was both thrilled and anxious, as I had never given an interview in my life. I had butterflies in my stomach. Without informing my parents, I headed out.

The office was in Thane, a northeastern suburb of Mumbai. I was told the easiest way to get there was by taking the local train, which is the lifeline of Mumbaikars, who travel daily from the suburbs to downtown to earn their livelihood. I had absolutely no idea what I was getting into.

Here I was in a metropolitan city which was not only big and complicated but also with millions of strangers around me. Though I was absolutely petrified and clueless, I knew that I had to be independent, and start my journey NOW!

It was Monday morning, and the city was bustling with office rush hour. Everybody was trying to get somewhere. I reached the metro station and got in the queue for tickets. At the counter, the stationmaster asked, "*Tumala Kuthe Jayeche Aahe.*" I was looking at the guy, puzzled because I didn't understand a word he said. Somebody from behind prompted, "He is asking, where do you want to go?" I said, "Thane Sir." I got the ticket, but now the next challenge was from which platform to board the train.

People in Mumbai are known to be helpful. A lady guided me on how to get to the platform and explained how I needed to change a few lines to get to my destination. It all sounded gibberish to me. Eventually, I mustered some courage and told myself, "I have to figure this out, and not let it wear me out."

I somehow managed to reach the place where I was being interviewed. At the end of it, I got an offer as the Product Manager. My first salary was a mere INR 8999 (less than USD 150) a month. I grabbed the opportunity with both hands.

The next challenge was to convince my parents to allow me to stay in Mumbai. I was sure my father would have shown resistance. But I managed to convince him by agreeing to stay at my cousin's place.

Now, houses in Mumbai are like matchboxes. There were already six people living in that tiny 1000 sq ft house. I barely had a place to fit myself in, let alone my things. I had to share a single bed with my cousin's sister. I wasn't exactly welcomed there, but I had to live with the odds. I couldn't have gone back to Vizag. This situation was a great testament to my resilience.

This carried on for more than a year, causing me immense distress. I was uncomfortable staying under such circumstances. I reached out to my parents, asking if I could move to a hostel. Yes, in India, we have to ask permission even at the age of 24, especially if you are not married. My father vetoed it.

This left me with two choices, either I get married or move back to Vizag. The latter was not an option for me. I got married in 1997 to my partner, against his will. We were too young to get married, and take on the responsibilities of running a household. But, we took the plunge. Despite initial teething issues, we managed it well. Things were finally working out.

After a few job changes, I found one at a leading jewellery firm, working as a Sales Manager for the US market. Though I knew nothing about the trade, I slogged my butt off for the next five years, learning everything about jewellery from scratch. I spent more than six months on the floor learning the fine nuances of jewellery making, understanding diamond grading, pricing structures, and business in general before I could actually sit in front of a client to conduct business or even communicate with them. I also got myself trained as a diamond certifier. There is no substitute for hard work.

In 2008 came an opportunity for my husband to move to Singapore to pursue his career. The Lion City is considered the safest city globally with zero percent crime and a great place to live. It was also a good opportunity for my three-year-old daughter's education.

Having said that, it was a tough decision to make as we had to uproot ourselves from India. I had to quit my job. My in-laws were living with us; we had to make the most difficult decision to shift them to another city and settle them down. Bearing the guilt of leaving behind ageing parents is never going to be easy.

Not completely oblivious to the worst Global Financial Crisis the world has ever faced, we took our chances in moving. It was going to be now or never.

Little did we know that things would start crumbling within 12 months of our move. People were losing jobs, and companies were getting wiped out. It was incredibly scary.

My husband decided to move back to his previous company, but the position was in Singapore. I was on a dependent's visa. I had to find work for myself as the market situation was unpredictable and precarious. And both of us had to earn to have a comfortable living. That year was stressful.

I was offered a job with a jewellery firm that involved extensive travel, long hours of work, and a stressful work environment. Though not ideal for my daughter, who was still little and adjusting to her new environment, I had no choice but to accept.

Due to differences in the workplace cultures of India and Singapore, I found it difficult to fit in. I was an outcast. I had to unlearn and relearn. It took me more than six months to be one of them. Slowly and steadily, I gained their confidence. I also had to adapt to the local culture, eating habits, and more passive ways to get things done.

Extensive travel created havoc in my daughter's life. I was living out of suitcases, travelled 200 days a year, and she missed her mommy. Each time I travelled, my guilt grew. It started affecting my performance. My husband had an equally hectic travel schedule. We would keep juggling our schedules to make sure at least one parent was around. There were times when our itineraries overlapped. An alternative arrangement had to be made for my daughter to stay at our friend's house.

This carried on for more than four years. As she grew older, it got tougher for her to comprehend the situation. She got more demanding. Ultimately I had to call it QUITS!

The break served me well. I was able to spend more time with my daughter. But a year into it, she didn't need me as much. My life seemed purposeless. I had to get back into the workforce, but I didn't want to return to the corporate world, as it would mean getting back into the same rut. That's when the entrepreneurial bug bit me. It also meant working on my own terms and having a better work-life balance. I was excited!

With an extensive trot across the globe, panning from South to North America, to Europe, Asia, and the Middle East, travel was always my thing and a big high for me. From there germinated the idea of starting an adventure travel company – Outwoods. It had a unique and exotic mix of adventure, photography, and the thrill of the wild. All in all, it was an ambitious dream project!

Little did I know what running a travel agency in Singapore entails. Apart from the huge investments, travel agency licenses, and yearly audits, it was a tough business to run. Soon funds began depleting, and expenses were rising. I had sleepless nights. I toiled for hours and hours to create itineraries, but nothing was working. The business was sporadic, and competition was fierce.

This went on for two years. Eventually, it became extremely difficult to keep the company afloat without pumping in more funds. My business partner was unwilling to contribute, and I didn't want my husband to fork out additional money to fund the company further. With a heavy heart and a deep sense of failure, I had to shut it down.

This took a toll on my health and mental condition. I couldn't come to terms with the failure and couldn't see the light at the end of the tunnel. For days I would lie in bed thinking, "What went wrong? Why did I fail? What next?" I felt depressed and dejected. But every morning, I would wake up and tell myself things would turn around, and they did.

In April 2016, another opportunity knocked on my door. I have always believed in the power of Karma. Do your bit, and things will come around. The Universe will make it happen.

My best friend was relocating to Hong Kong. She needed someone for the business continuity of her Event Management Company in Singapore. For years, I supported her as a trusted friend during various events she had been organising. Now, she asked me if I would like to come on board as a partner, officially. Perhaps it was an obvious decision for her. But for me, this was a game-changer!

It couldn't have been better timing. Though I was sad to see my friend leave, I knew this was an opportunity for both of us to make this company bigger with offices in two countries.

Since then, there has been no looking back. With complementary skill sets and an aligned vision, there was no stopping us. Sure, we have had our share of ups and downs, but we have grown, and are known as the KIT KAT Team. It's been five years, and we have grown from strength to strength.

I have had my own set of failures, struggles, and challenges. But one shouldn't be perturbed by these obstacles; instead, face them head-on with full zeal and determination.

I have learnt more from my failures than from my successes. It has made me more resilient, determined, and enduring in facing the challenges.

Moving forward, I wish to leave a legacy for my daughter, who can be proud of her mother for being strong, independent emotionally, and financially. We should empower our kids, especially daughters, to become strong individuals and be fearless to face the world. I will always be grateful that my mom wanted me to be strong and independent. I hope I can inculcate the same values in my daughter.

The COVID-19 pandemic has taught me life will continue to be tough and unpredictable, and with the current bizarre times, change is inevitable. We have to be more adaptable and re-calibrate our personal and professional life to remain relevant and purposeful.

This is my story. What's yours?

About The Author

Shikha Sarkar, Managing Partner & Director at Kit Kat Events & Marketing and Co-Founder of Global Influencers Publishing House, has more than 20 years of experience in international sales and marketing across various industries. Adding to the mixture her strong entrepreneurial skills, she knows what it takes to make things work. Shikha is a steely, determined and passionate person, with a strong inclination to take up new adventures and challenges that come her way.

For the last five years, she has been the Ambassador of InterNations, one of the largest global expat networks, supporting a dynamic community of over 60,000 expats from 200 different countries living in Singapore.

Shikha has always been passionate about empowering and uplifting women. In keeping with her work in this area she recently joined as a Fundraiser Volunteer for MITU (Multiple Initiatives Towards Upliftment) helping disadvantaged girls and women with issues related to menstrual hygiene, skilling, and up-cycling in India.

Shikha can be contacted at:

Email: *shikha@globalinfluencers.sg*

LinkedIn: *https://www.linkedin.com/in/shikhasarkar/*

Website: *www.globalinfluencers.sg*

STORY EIGHTEEN

The Beauty of Crossroads

A ship in harbour is safe, but that is not what ships are built for.

We humans have a strange love affair with planning! Even while believing in philosophies like "God Willing," "Insha'Allah," and "pre-written destinies," consciously or not, we plan. We envision our lives to turn out in a particular way, and from then on, it seems our entire DNA is hard-wired towards the sole purpose of achieving this vision.

We define success, set patterns, and establish our "normal" based on this, and attempt, sometimes at any cost, to maintain this self-designed equilibrium. Hence, it's not surprising that crossroads are difficult, at times even detrimental, because this doesn't condition us for change. We start believing in the plan more than we do in ourselves. And ironically, the very plan we design to achieve our vision, ends up becoming our Achilles heel.

There have been many crossroads in my journey! Each shaped me in unique ways and offered new opportunities, but I didn't register these earlier. Instead, I fought it! I was the master of my destiny. I had achieved my plan so far, sometimes with incredible difficulty, which just fuelled my belief that if I had the will, there was a way. I didn't reflect, rethink my vision, redefine success or explore alternative paths. At every crossroad, I just worked harder on what I already knew to stay on course.

2015 marked an important crossroad for my career, which changed the way I looked at crossroads altogether. Little had I envisioned that the year would mark the sudden death of my corporate life. One which I'd carefully curated since high school.

Could I have resuscitated my corporate life? Yes, had I taken the logical next step of another corporate role, but why was my heart revolting against this seemingly sensible option?

Instead of exciting, these roles felt more like a cage. The thought of turning up to the same office every day, doing the same thing, and more importantly not being able to do the many other things I suddenly desired and felt were important, wore me out even before I'd started.

What was I looking for? Not being able to answer this question, I asked others. Had I retired? Was I done?

In stark contrast to these questions, I felt I had more in me, not less! I wanted to do many things, but I craved impact more. I wanted to create value, but more importantly deliver value. I wanted to do different things and do things differently… and… I wanted to do them on my terms!

This rising passion for all things new and different clashed with my safe old world, and this nagging discontent became a catalyst for my new trajectory.

Growing up, the expectations of me were no different to many others. Finish your studies, get a degree, find a stable job, get married and start a family (hopefully in that order). So, I set out to achieve this (but not in this order).

Armed with my international business degree, I worked in interesting companies and roles. Starting in research and analytics, I moved to consumer goods as their youngest regional manager and then to the wonderful world of hospitality to set up and head different functions.

These companies gave me opportunities to learn, develop my knowledge, skills, and experience, and most enjoyably, travel. I had great colleagues and some amazing bosses.

My plan seemed to have worked, so why was I so disconnected now?

As I reflected, I wasn't surprised that I'd been quite entrepreneurial most of my life. I knew this about myself. In primary school, I was organising fairs to raise money for the basic needs of our class and classmates. In high school, I was in the student council trying to bring about change.

All my corporate roles were peppered with entrepreneurial elements that I either volunteered for or was tasked with. I was part of teams that created new research tools and the first developing markets innovation pipeline. I had set up new capabilities, created new brands and programs and co-founded a company to invest in early-stage ideas and learn from the start-up community.

What did surprise me was I seemed to have driven more social impact earlier in my life. Now, while I was still entrepreneurial and driving change, it was mostly financial rather than social.

I had seen my grandparents and parents do an immense amount of social work. I had the same genes, which were now fighting not to remain dormant.

I supported social causes passively with donations, but my corporate "busyness" and fatigue made it difficult to engage beyond this. Similarly, I was a passive player in the start-up world, where I invested financially but didn't engage nor learn as I'd planned.

The immense sense of personal satisfaction that comes from making a real difference was missing, masked by the recognition that came with creating new and shiny things.

The reflections made me realise that it was not just the "*what*" I was doing but the "*how*" I was doing it that truly made me feel accomplished, content, and happy. And I had long credited and valued the "*where*" I was, for being responsible for all of this.

No wonder I was struggling to fit all that would make me happy into another role.

Entrepreneurialism and innovation would remain integral pillars, but social impact and the start-up world needed to play bigger roles in my new world. I also knew I needed to earn, not just to support my family but also for financial independence and a lifestyle, but not at the cost of the freedom, space, and time with my family that I valued.

This only meant one thing. I had to build the kind of life I wanted.

This idea both excited and terrified me. My rational and emotional energies had never been in this much conflict before. As much energy as I put into fanning my passion, an equal amount (if not more) went into worrying about our financial commitments, my abilities, and fighting the "imposter syndrome."

Embarking on a start-up had so many risks, both real and perceived. It was not reassuring to read statistics that showed 90% of start-ups fail, 75% of venture-backed start-ups fail, and that the information industry had the highest failure rate. Founder resilience and fatigue were the biggest reasons for these failures. I had to have faith in myself and resilience to do this.

"A ship in harbour is safe, but that is not what ships are built for"! This quote sent by my sister was the final push I needed to chart a new course and set sail.

While I was less fussed about most corporate trappings, I was afraid of not having support. I hated admin and finance. I was terrified I didn't know sales and of the idea of cold calling (which, for some reason, is what I thought I'd be doing). It was also tough to deal with sentiments like, "*You have always been a client, are you sure you can consult, it requires you to do the work?* "*As a woman, how will you juggle all this?*"...or "*So you're really the boss?*"... or my personal favourite... "*Does your husband approve?*"

I had never been afraid of new or unknown areas. It had been a large part of my role, and I enjoyed it. However, in my corporate roles I didn't question my abilities to thrive because I had an infrastructure to support me. Benjamin Franklin and many others have been strong proponents of preparation, *"By failing to prepare, you are preparing to fail."* Following this motto, I set about building a support network to tackle areas I couldn't or didn't want to do.

Thinking we must know it and do it all (like I did) isn't the smartest strategy for success. Asking for help isn't a sign of weakness, and the power of collaboration cannot be underestimated. I always believed that if I couldn't do whatever was asked of me, it meant that I didn't know how to do my job. I've had bosses who made me feel this, and this was perhaps the toughest, yet the most liberating learning of all.

It was against this backdrop that I took the first of many tentative steps towards building a new life with my first two projects. One for a large multinational and another for an NGO that I admired greatly and Lexicon, a management consulting agency, and TRIBE, a social enterprise, were born.

With Lexicon, I took on corporate projects, allowing me to stay connected to the industries I loved, work on global challenges, and check off financial goals, while TRIBE allowed me to fulfil my desire for social impact.

Over time TRIBE's social conscience made its way into my consulting world, as I started to enable corporations and brands with building stronger social purposes, amplifying the social impact I desired to create.

The biggest thing to overcome in any crossroad is dealing with uncertainty and I had a huge amount. In my corporate life, I never thought about my pay cheque. It was a given. Starting my own consultancy meant I had no gauge of my monthly revenue, or how to manage this uncertainty while planning for growth and expansion. I had to learn how to plan with many unknown variables, but it is just a matter of time when patterns start to emerge amidst the chaos.

While I had to learn new skills, I also had to unlearn and correct an even larger number of skills and perceptions, especially about myself.

I was thrust into the world of business development to build a new network and a new brand. As extroverted as I am, I felt business development wasn't my thing. I was used to dealing with strategy, delivering factual insights and objective performance results, and I had lots of preconceived perceptions of sales.

Today, it is one of the things I enjoy the most in my day. I thoroughly enjoy meeting new and different people, listening to their amazing stories and experiences, discussing a variety of business challenges, and collaborating on solutions.

While all this may seem like a lot to contend with, I surprisingly found myself with time. I no longer had the shackles of copious amounts of calls and meetings, administration, and so many other process tasks that occupied a corporate day.

I had time to focus on my angel investment and TRIBE and plan how to make a stronger impact with both, build two brands, set up programmes, and develop partnerships in quite a few countries around the region. This ability to do more and still have time was such an energy boost. It makes you feel that you can take on the world.

Since Lexicon and TRIBE were established, they have flourished, but nothing is without its ups and downs. 2020 was my toughest year yet. While I had to learn to adapt and look for new opportunities, I also benefited from partnerships I had built and the social goodwill I had accumulated. Kindness and collaboration are extremely strong and often under-utilised forces.

Thinking back to my decision to leave the corporate world, would I change anything? Yes, but only one. I wish I had done it earlier. I held on to something for a little bit longer than I should have because I didn't believe in my own abilities. I also enjoyed my corporate career immensely, it set me up for what I do today, but I believe things are not right or wrong indefinitely. They are right in the right phase of your life.

Are there times when my heart says something, and my brain says the opposite? Yes … but at these crossroads, the decision is mine to make.

It is absolutely possible to assemble all the elements that make you happy and build the kind of life you truly desire. It takes a little creativity, belief in yourself and the resilience to stay the course and of course the support of your loved ones.

If my journey inspires even one reader to live "their version of the best life", then I have done my part.

About The Author

Roshni Pandey is the Co-Founder of BlueBox, an investment and advisory group nurturing and developing early-stage ideas. She's the Founder and Managing Partner of Lexicon, a management consulting firm enabling organisations to navigate increasingly dynamic trading environments and drive new growth through creative strategy and innovation.

Roshni has worked across global agencies, MNCs, various regions and industries and held senior management roles centred on building and delivering new value. She's a firm believer in the balance between art and science; intuition and data, and profit and purpose.

Her passion for social causes has seen her launch several initiatives. FutureWise, a skills acquisition program and TRIBE, is a social enterprise enabling children and women from underserved communities in Asia Pacific.

She is a judge for Women of the Future awards, providing young women recognition for their achievements and the winner of several awards.

Roshni can be contacted at:

Email: *roshni@bluebox.com.sg*

LinkedIn: *https://www.linkedin.com/in/roshnipandey/*

Website: *https://www.bluebox.com.sg/*

STORY NINETEEN

The Journey of Authenticity

The turning point was coming to the truth that I did not need my mother to embrace my authenticity

Growing up in a loving home with my parents and siblings was something that I will always be grateful for. The environment was warm, nurturing and allowed me to be who I wanted to be. I could do foolish things, ask questions if I did not understand, and just be myself around my family. Yes, I am almost certain that my parents did not understand this very inquisitive child who wished only to do things that made sense to her, no matter what the expectations were in the world. As much as they allowed this freedom of expression, it was still foreign to them. It was something that they were learning as they were going along. When they were young, children did as they were told and did not ask many questions.

I can comfortably say that, for the most part, my parents were not stuck in their old ways, albeit it surfaced occasionally. The challenges, however, came as soon as I stepped outside this very safe home environment. Things were different outside, and the world was cruel, very judgmental, and intolerant. In primary school, I was bullied and did not know how to stand up for myself. My authentic self was suppressed and frowned upon. The sad thing is you end up doing what is expected of you, what society deems acceptable and morally correct.

True to my family tradition, I was sent to boarding school when I started high school. I was 12 at the time. I exploited that as an opportunity to start afresh and emerge from my protective shell. I used the new school, new environment, and new society as an opportunity to redefine myself – or rather reconnect with my true self, my authentic self.

Was this my voice coming out? Did I suddenly have the freedom to express myself the way I wanted to? Having to repress your authenticity in any way is like being suffocated. It is as if your whole being is under a heavy rock, and no matter how much you try and push this rock over, your efforts bear no fruit.

It was as if the Universe was aligning with my goals when I met and made friends with two super confident girls. They did not need affirmation from anyone and were so true to themselves. I knew I had to stick to the friendship if I were to realise my goal of living authentically.

The five years that I spent at boarding school were my very best years. I learnt to peel off every layer of hiding and shame. I discovered so much about myself, about my potential, my abilities, and my developmental areas. I immersed myself in the things that mattered and helped me to fully nurture and enhance my skills.

It was a real blessing that the school I attended also focused on developing well-rounded leaders and not only on academics. When I completed high school, I was confident that I was now ready for the big world and all its challenges. To my surprise, I was about to find out that the hurdles had just begun, and I still had so much to learn.

Going to university meant going to the big city. Just when I thought I had full control of myself, understanding my authentic self, and having gained the confidence to live authentically, arriving in the big city felt like I had to start the process all over again. It was another dimension of the discovery process that required a bigger resilience and emotional maturity. I needed to bring a different mindset and attitude to the challenge. I was only 17 when I arrived in Johannesburg, and I had to refer to the same coping skills that I used when I started boarding school, albeit at a higher level.

The third phase was when I started in the corporate world. If I thought that coming to the big city was a challenge that required me to step up, going into the corporate world was something else totally.

Nothing could have entirely prepared me for what I was about to experience. The battle lines were blurred in this corporate beast, and it would be quite easy to lose oneself as you try and navigate this gigantic maze.

Everything that I had learnt about myself was challenged. It was as if I was expected to strip myself and become a whole new person. How was I to survive this very unpredictable world with so many conflicting expectations? What references do I have to navigate this one? I found myself in a perpetual whirlwind.

I saw people struggle against a system that seemed to exclude and side line them, irrespective of their experience, qualifications, and valuable contributions. It was very discouraging to see the people I looked up to, get swallowed by this very debilitating system. On the other side, it fired up my fighting spirit to rely on my own confidence and abilities.

During this time, I leant on my mother a lot. My mother was always my go-to person. She had all the answers when I felt that it was all becoming too overwhelming for me. The corporate world required me to dig deeper than I had ever done to access places in my being that unlocked the tenacity to deal with it all. I had to find my true north to guide my navigation. In retrospect, however, I was still only surviving and had left the pursuit to thrive behind. The self-work had completely stopped amid just trying to survive.

The Penny Drops

In 2011, my mother passed away, and it suddenly felt like I was all alone. My mother was now just a distant memory and a point of reference. During the counselling journey, it dawned on me that I had unconsciously been hiding in my mother's shadow; what she taught me as a young girl, how to behave in the world, how to find solutions for problems, how to approach certain situations etc. But, how could that be when I had always been such an independent young girl?

I mean, I have always had a mind of my own and seldom conformed to standards set by society. I have always had a clear vision of how I want my life to turn out, and none of those were attached to my mother.

The biggest gift, however, came in the realisation that the safety net that my mother was to me disempowered me to boldly and unapologetically take a stand to be authentically me in the world where there are many expectations of how one should behave, talk, walk, dress, express their views – especially as a woman.

I had to learn to fully express myself without fear and without the comfort of having my mother to turn to should things go pear-shaped. The turning point was, coming to the truth that I did not need my mother to embrace my authenticity.

I learnt that my authenticity was not tied to her in any way. I had to tap deep inside the core of my being to connect with that authenticity. I had to do the work of understanding it, cultivating it, owning it, and then fully embracing it.

This was certainly the most liberating and fulfilling thing that I had ever done in my life. I could almost smell and feel what it is like to have true meaning in life. How could I have missed it all along? It sadly had to take my mother's passing for me to realise this beautiful truth and then live it.

Stepping Into My Truth Authentically

This big discovery of my authenticity unleashed so much power that I never imagined I had within me. I had to spend so much time with myself, reflecting and thinking about all the things that I could now do since I had found this beautiful gift. I oozed confidence like never before.

After all, at its core, authenticity is about knowing, accepting, and remaining true to oneself. I was suddenly bold enough to speak up on the issues that bothered me. I could connect with myself on a much deeper level, a spiritual elevation almost. I was freer in my thinking, in my engagements with others, and in putting myself out there.

I was not afraid of anything, not even of being vulnerable. I had the courage to be involved in difficult conversations that people generally shy away from. I developed the muscle to boldly speak my mind and articulate my thoughts with audacity.

Fully Living With Authenticity

As I continue the journey of authenticity and self-development, I step into the world proud of who I am and what I imbue. I have no reservations about my capabilities and the things that I can achieve, my influence, and the spaces that I occupy. Focusing on myself gave me back control of my own life, as it should be.

Once you do this, you become unapologetic about who you are, and what you are about. It becomes so liberating that you become numb to other people's thoughts and opinions about you, and their absurd expectations of you, and generally your choices in life.

I now stand on stages and question how many women are pressured to adapt to male-dominated leadership styles. I question how men are still dominating boardrooms and key decision making. I question how the playgrounds are not level for promotional opportunities for both men and women, and it bothers me that some women are still shying away from making the transformational shift to make an impact.

I advocate for mentoring young people to provide both social and professional support. I question how women are made to feel insecure and less confident in their roles as leaders.

I challenge the traditional masculine culture in many corporate organisations, which results in female leaders being overlooked for promotions, and stretch opportunities that promote the advancement of female leaders.

I now use coaching as an effective tool to assist me in this journey of personal development.

Through coaching, individuals may go through a process of self-discovery and therefore live out their authentic selves. This becomes liberating because we get to know exactly what we can be and do and what we can never be.

We get to lead from an authentic self and therefore meaningfully influence others. We get to discover our purpose in life and become more deliberate in realising that purpose.

I believe that there is a burning desire deep inside of all of us (at the very core of our being) that drives us to pursue something in life. I help individuals consciously become aware of the thing or things that make them feel great, challenge them to spend a significant amount of time doing the things that energise them, and sharpen their skills by learning techniques that help them be best.

I have created a platform that is focused on having nonconventional dialogues that are necessary to start making transformational changes. Have deep conversations around the issues of leadership and authenticity.

I urge every girl and woman who reads this to develop the confidence to own their space and challenge things that do not sit well with them.

You have to activate the power that you have, and be fearless in pursuing your own purpose. Do not live, nor be defined by, anyone else's expectations of you.

Set your own standards, find your passion, be consistent in your pursuit for success, know your worth and make an impact.

About The Author

Thato Belang is a zealous inspirational, keynote and TEDx Speaker, a Leadership and Authenticity Coach, and Facilitator. Her research on Business Executive Coaching and female leaders' authenticity, has made her a guru on the subject of authenticity.

She is passionate about people development and growth, leadership development, African problem-solving, storytelling and has experience in the Financial Services, Telecommunications, Mining, and Insurance industries.

Thato systematically works with individuals to help use their authenticity as their power to influence and make an impact. This passion has led her to become a member of the Female Wave of Change; a global movement that unites women changing the world into a better place.

She has also created a platform called Authentic Dialogues with Thato where relevant, compelling, engaging and inspiring conversations take place in a manner that shifts perspectives and propel people to serve, positively influence and make an impact in the world.

Thato can be contacted at:

Email: *thato.belang@gmail.com*

LinkedIn: *https://www.linkedin.com/in/thato-belang-73755a9/*

Facebook: *https://www.facebook.com/thato.belang*

STORY TWENTY

The Return to Self

When you want more but you're scared, don't stop! What you fear today becomes your comfort zone tomorrow.

I'm among the last to walk into the meeting room at one of our largest operational centres. I placed my latte on the oval table and sat down, smiling nervously as introductions are made: Director of Technology, Director of Operations...

As I observe my well-spoken colleagues, with their superior intellect and qualifications, I anticipate the arrival of the talent investigators, coming to remove me from my role.

How did I get here?

My average degree from an average university, a northern English accent, which I believed sounded common and inarticulate, and my lack of international experience, were all evidence that I was not worthy of a European Director role, big salary, house by the sea, cream Mini Cooper with brown leather interior and more money in my account than I needed.

At 24, I couldn't go back to my parents because I'd moved away from home, alone, to build a "career." I'd left my family and friends for a city I knew nothing about, a team leader position and a measly pay rise, all in anticipation of the opportunities that would follow.

For several years, my bank account was overdrawn. My "career" and critically needed house renovations were at a standstill, and my old VW Polo was not in great shape.

The appointment of an inspiring new leader at work, an outstanding communicator with strong values, and a powerful vision got me fired up. Finally, someone I could learn from.

Lesson 1: Study the attributes of people doing well at the things you want to do.

At 9, I was accepted into a swimming squad. I was small and slow, but as I paddled alongside swimmers effortlessly gliding through the water, I studied their techniques, and I got better, fast!

When I watched swimmers and adopted their techniques, I became a better swimmer. When I studied our new leader, I became a better leader. I observed his behaviour, how he made decisions, and how he engaged people, grateful to have him as a role model.

A company restructure created two senior leadership positions and two management positions. Of 25 team leaders only two of us were being considered for both levels. My peers congratulated me, believing, as I did, that whatever happened, a promotion was on the cards.

I had been unhappy to leave the town and the people I loved, but at last, it was going to be worth it! I picked out my company car and redesigned my kitchen.

After the assessment process, I was invited into one of the glass-walled rooms that framed the edges of the open-plan office to be told that I had failed the assessment process and was not suitable for *either* role! Humiliated and distraught, I hid my face so the people outside, waiting for the news, wouldn't see me crying.

Lesson 2: Choose your attitude carefully.

A mentor said, "Everyone will be waiting to see how you react."

I made it my mission to leap into my "development project" with an awesome attitude. I passionately supported the new leadership team and delivered great results.

Lesson 3: Find the good in every situation (regardless of how challenging things may seem).

Focus your attention on what's good and ask yourself a daily power question, for example: *Why am I easily bringing the best version of myself every day?*

After a couple of years, despite my expanding knowledge and technical qualifications, I was no closer to a real seat at the leadership table or more money.

Lesson 4: To achieve a breakthrough, you must be willing to *do* things differently.

Your results are largely determined by the action you take or fail to take. What action *could* you take today that would improve your results? Isolate these actions and try to identify what's holding you back so that you can address the barriers and make the progress you desire.

I started studying the habits of elite performers and applied them immediately. I'd begin each day with exercise, practice gratitude, set intentions, focus on my goals, and feed my mind with empowering and inspiring ideas.

In a surge of confidence, I posted my CV on a recruitment website. A tentative peek into the possibilities outside my company of nine years set in motion a stunning chain of events.

Within a week, I was called by a recruiter inviting me to interview for a European Management position. I walked into the lobby of a local hotel to meet the person who would become my boss and mentor.

Lesson 5: Imagine your most brilliant self, and bring that person to every situation.

I was like an Olympic athlete at the starting blocks of the 100 metres sprint, having trained four years for this moment! I was passionate, yet poised, animated, yet authentic.

We connected instantly! Within twenty minutes, he offered me the role, double my salary, a company car, and a management bonus scheme!

Shaking, I told him I'd think about it and left the hotel, literally not believing what had just happened. Twenty-four hours later, the recruiter called to invite me to a second meeting.

Once again, I shook his hand and sat across from him in the hotel lobby. He offered me the European Director position and wrote an even higher number on a piece of paper. Almost speechless, trembling, smiling, and trying to act cool, I accepted.

Mediocre talent, modest beginnings, average intellect, and a reserved personality, but I had persisted.

Lesson 6: Persist, *with ease*

Keep your mind light yet focused and take continuous action towards your desires, holding them in your mind with unshakable belief, but not impatience.

There is only one brilliant you, and you are on this planet for your own, very unique reason. Have faith in the idea that the path of your greatest joy will unfold for you.

Under the guidance of an amazing mentor, I gained confidence, was shortlisted for leader of the year, and within two years, my salary had increased by another 40%! I was given a bigger remit reporting directly to the CEO, a short-lived crest, before a massive disappointment.

Following a merger, I'd been working under a new leader for a few months. One Friday afternoon, he informed me of a big global role they had created for me and enthusiastically referred me to his counterpart in America for the details.

She started to talk about my talents and fit for a new global role in business development, and I felt excited about the promotion. But when she floated an organisational chart in front of me, I felt the blow to my gut. The job was two levels below my current position, reporting to a manager in America!

Hurting, I felt tricked and let down. My American leader was astonished when I respectfully told her that I would be resigning.

I drove home in tears of frustration, and when my phone rang, I pulled over to the side of the road. She was deeply apologetic and asked me to remain as a Director in the European executive team and accept the new role. I thanked her, agreed, assured her of my full commitment (and meant it), and hung up.

On my last day, I sent an email to the organisation thanking them for their support, acknowledging their talents, and wishing them and the company well.

With every promotion came a fresh wave of self-doubt, which started to reduce once I'd banked some good results.

Lesson 7: Aim to do work that feels beyond who you are today.

I've learned that life is about growth. We get stuck because we can't *see* ourselves being or doing anything else.

If you're not currently doing the thing you love, identify one small action you can take today that moves you toward it. Repeat this tomorrow, and the next day, and the next...

Go for ventures that *require* you to become bigger than who you currently are so that you can release your talents into the world.

Lesson 8: Visualise and feel yourself achieving the things you want.

Occasionally I am asked whether being a woman has ever held me back. Perhaps naively, until my penultimate leadership role, I'd never thought about it.

I was struggling to build a relationship with one of the four Managing Directors I supported. My team delivered projects in his market, and at least once a week, he emailed me with complaints, copying in our boss. I'd call him, take the red-eye flight to meet with him in person, doing everything in my power to address his concerns, but it was never enough. As I resolved one issue, a new grievance would follow.

In the airport, over coffee, I shared my frustration with a colleague, telling him that I didn't know what else to do. This was an important market for our company, my partnership with this Managing Director was important, and I was failing. My colleague thought for a second before answering, "Have you ever considered that it might just be good old-fashioned chauvinism and that nothing you say or do will make a difference?"

Breakthrough! It had never crossed my mind!

Lesson 9: Hear the opinions of others, but hold them gently.

I continued to make the required improvements to turn the results around, but I stopped trying to please him, releasing some of the burden from my shoulders.

Trying to avoid criticism and satisfy everyone was a dangerous theme for me, rooted in the idea that I was not worthy of a six-figure salary and an executive role.

When I became an entrepreneur, I had to address this. Today, I show my clients how to invite and welcome the discomfort of exploring new terrain.

I was uncertain about my talent, intellect, and potential, but somehow my desire for results and progress was always stronger than my doubts.

Remember that it is normal to feel scared when you do something new. Don't see this as a sign that you're not capable, confident, or good enough. Keep going, knowing that what you fear today, becomes your comfort zone tomorrow.

I'd had the best time as a VP at American Express Global Business Travel, leading the integration of two global companies. I started exploring how big visions get created and achieved, studying human potential and team performance.

It was intensive and hugely challenging. I was working with amazing people, and we were energised and aligned behind our big goals. Being away from home every week was hard on my family, and I was exhausted, but I was totally confident, calm, and in control.

I'd started to understand myself on a deeper level, hushing my intellectual mind to release more emotion and creativity.

Ironically, I'd finally found my groove as an executive, right before I left it all behind to become an entrepreneur!

On a hot August evening, during a family holiday in Spain, I told my extended family that I'd be leaving my big job to start my own business.

I'd made the decision months ago but announcing it created the oddest and unexpected feeling, like a hot air balloon, weightlessness and liberated as it is released into the sky, to be steered by the wind.

Perhaps you have an idea of something you want to experience beyond where you are today. Please know that if you make a committed decision to go for it, it will happen. Release yourself from the thought that the path to the things you want must be known in advance.

I am deeply grateful that the past 40 years have been perfectly preparing me for my new mission to help hundreds of thousands of people improve the quality of their life.

Lesson 10: Live in gratitude.

Whatever you're spending your time on right now, be grateful for it, give it everything you've got while working towards your "next" purpose.

It can be anything you want it to be. What will yours be?

About The Author

Lorna Dunning is a Success Coach who has helped countless people improve the quality of their personal and professional lives through her seminars, coaching programmes, articles and her online community #BeTheChange.

Spending 20 years in multinational organisations, working alongside talented professionals, provided Lorna with deep insights into the methods and mindsets of high-performance individuals, leading rich and rewarding lives.

A few years ago, Lorna said farewell to her executive leadership career to devote herself fully to her passion for helping others achieve limitless success and fulfilment in all parts of their lives. She also helps teams to thrive, think big, work together and achieve bold outcomes!

Both Lorna and her clients haven't looked back.

"Lorna is inspirational...she is totally invested in her client's success."

Lorna can be contacted at:

Email: *lorna@lornadunning.co.uk*

LinkedIn: *https://www.linkedin.com/in/lornadunning/*

Website: *www.lornadunning.co.uk*

STORY TWENTY ONE

The Unbound Eagle

I have never failed, just learnt 100 different ways of doing the same thing.

Early Years – Inspiration from my Mother

The time is 11:56 am, and the date, 27 September 1997. At that moment, it began! My life!

Nature, science, or a Divine being had conspired to present to Justine Aki, a teacher, and Albert Aki, an agronomist, with their third jewel...their third daughter.

My siblings and I were raised in a loving Christian home with strong values of hard work, humanity, and discipline, which have shaped and continue to guide us.

Among the earliest memories I have of my parents are of them telling my older sisters that they had all it took to be whatever they wanted to be. They made them sing songs and recite poems to that effect. Because of the frequency of the singing and recitals, I quickly got the hang of it, and that mantra organically became my guiding mantra.

Confidence was a key value in our household. In later conversations with my mother, she told me that she was very intentional about the upbringing of her children. She mentioned that she was keen on identifying their strengths at an early age and nurturing them.

At age six, I joined the Scout Movement, where I developed teamwork, leadership, and communication skills.

When I was ten years old, I joined the St John Ambulance as a *Badger* and became a *Cadet* in 2010. I acquired skills in First Aid and emergency response.

I wanted to be a doctor when I grew up but, at age 12, journalism came to mind. I wanted to be like Winnie Mukami, but my stammering got my classmates and teachers making fun and discouraging me because, to them, this was a disability.

My mother impressed me with a positive attitude, guided me until I overcame my weakness, and excelled in interpersonal relations and public speaking.

Self Discipline and Hardwork

Secondary school at a boarding school taught me the responsibility of taking charge of my life and greater self-awareness. My desire to become a doctor saw me take up biology, chemistry, physics, and mathematics.

To balance academics and co-curricular activities, I perfected being organised for holistic development in school. I became a leader in the Scout Movement while in Form 2, leading a troop to national competitions at Nairobi's Rowallan Camp. The leadership and teamwork skills acquired in primary school had come in handy.

Home Economics classes ignited a love for many things, including caring for the sick, bringing my dream of becoming a doctor closer.

Sometimes, during holidays, I saw my mum break down following harassment from relatives. This greatly fuelled my desire for Women's Rights Advocacy. The strong patriarchal culture of my society has obviously made it very difficult. That I personally experienced discrimination as a girl strengthened my resolve to never give up until I succeed.

After my "O" level exams in 2015, I spent 2016 with my mum in Bungoma. Staying with my mum showed me her highs and lows. Being there for her strengthened our mother-daughter bond.

She instilled in me the inextinguishable determination to excel as I appreciated how our parents shielded us from a lot. I began to see how harsh the world is.

This pre-university period laid the foundation for my future. I buried myself in volunteer work, started a business, and made life-changing decisions. Unable to find a scout unit in my area, I joined the Kenya Red Cross to engage in community work.

My first day with the Red Cross in Bungoma took me to Captain Mt. Elgon, where we rescued an eight-year-old child from a river. It had rained hard, and we had to trek a long way up the mountain. As the rain poured down, we sought shelter from a woman who lived in a structure made from maize stalks tucked into a tree. She had three children.

I took an interest in her plight and learnt of her struggles. The nearest market centre and school were five kilometres away. During the rains, her children skipped school because the makeshift bridge would be unstable and too risky to use.

Back at the office, I compiled my report then tried to follow up on the lady's case but failed to deliver my promise to help her. This sense of helplessness furthered my interest in Community Service.

As a volunteer, I undertook various activities to alleviate human suffering and put a smile on people's faces. I was the Assistant Youth Leader of the schools' outreach programs which launched Red Cross Clubs in secondary schools.

At the local pediatric hospital, I spent time "illegally" alongside my doctor friends, enhancing my First Aid skills by helping during ambulance responses and medical camps. This made me feel like the Universe was aligned to make me a Doctor.

My mother was now successful in business, and the bug bit me. I raised my first capital from the stipend I earned from volunteering with the Red Cross to start my first business – selling designer men's shirts, jewelry, and women's shoes. My mum would accompany me to Kenya's border with Uganda, where we bought and sold goods.

Without any business training and being consumed in teenage euphoria, I spent the profits on non-essentials. I lacked a clear spending plan, the business failed, and the money was lost. As much as it was frustrating to fail, I learnt to embrace and learn from it. After all, I have never failed, just learnt 100 different ways of doing the same thing.

I passed my secondary school exams but not well enough to join medical school. I explored other medical-related courses in vain. All options proved difficult.

My parents suggested I take another degree then pursue medicine later. My sisters, already in university, advised me to choose a passion-driven career and something that was marketable.

I chose a BA in Sociology, Political Science and Conflict, and Peace Studies at the University of Nairobi - East and Central Africa's most prestigious University.

University Years - Local and Global Experiences

University life was interesting! It was strange that I was not taking medicine, but I had to be focused and disciplined. My mum and sisters constantly advised, sometimes to the point of "lecturing" me to have my priorities right.

I rejoined the Scout Movement in my first week at the university. Being outspoken and having a strong personality rubbed some people the wrong way.

Negativity notwithstanding, I was nominated as a Sub-County Youth Leader. I was a little nervous and sought my Troop Leader's advice, and he told me to "do what you think is right."

In standing for what I considered the scouting values – learning by doing – I was frustrated by senior students and leaders who did not respect my position because I was their junior. I was the only woman leading a team of four.

In September 2018, I represented Kenya at the Africa Scout Youth Forum in Zimbabwe and participated in the International Leadership Training event in Burundi.

Earlier in 2017, I had been part of Educate! – a social enterprise network aimed at transforming education in Africa, as one of several pioneer mentors. We learnt business, pitching, facilitation, and how to mentor students into leadership while developing their entrepreneurial skills.

I got to mentor high school students and train youths in underserved communities on entrepreneurship. This is how I met my life coach and mentor. Being mentored and guided into my professional life by friends and a mentor has been and continues to be the cornerstone of my growth.

The experience at Educate! awakened my passion for business. Having had chest problems during our high school camps, I resorted to selling duvets with aesthetic value to keep users warm and prevent chest complications like I had.

Business boomed! I started saving money to pay my bills at the University, taking the burden off my parents. I even used a percentage of savings to support a children's home in my village.

In 2018, I travelled across Africa as a scout and young change maker, the exposure to different cultures and realities on the African continent highly motivating me. In the Scout Movement, I coordinated events, trained youth on critical skills to expose them to the labor market. I started the Ankara Notebooks Project to enable female students to develop entrepreneurship and financial literacy skills to build financial independence.

We were transforming perceived waste into valuable items in line with SDG 13-Climate Action. The project excelled at the Scouts Centenary Camp and drew huge interest.

Then came the 2018 Africa Basque Challenge – a week-long boot camp for teams of 40 young innovators from Spain, DRC, Somalia, and Kenya to collaborate in creating solutions to challenges and overcome barriers to their goals. I talked about my entrepreneurial experience, after which I received a scholarship to the University of Mondragon in Bilbao, Spain.

Nothing had prepared me for the culture shock that awaited me in Spain. Their individualistic lifestyle was so different to what I was used to, and the language barrier meant I used Google translator.

It was initially uncomfortable to be stared at everywhere, sometimes experiencing racism openly. Some people would run away when I approached them to ask for directions. Their food was different, and it was not easy adjusting to pinchos, etc.

To make ends meet, I got a teaching job at the Miribilla School. Juggling between school and English teaching was a challenge. The hard life in Spain was worthwhile.

I joined the University of Mondragon four months late, but their unique project-based learning model was exciting to me, so I settled in quite fast. My only frustration was that the Africa-related projects I initiated failed because most of my team members had neither been to nor had much knowledge about Africa.

Nevertheless, I had to hang on. I was elected leader for my team company and later served as the CEO. This helped me learn several lessons about leadership. That while leadership can be lonely and energy-sapping, standing with others is critical. Time spent in uncomfortable zones is when you grow.

Early in 2020, I travelled to the USA for a six-month academic experience, working on the Hex6 Sustainable Fashion brand, which I co-founded. We had meetings, developed networks and markets, held a fashion event, and were doing great before COVID-19 happened and I had to travel to Kenya.

While back home, we got going with my university team by online learning.

My mum fell sick at this time and needed attention. I last saw her in January and needed to travel to Western Kenya to be with her. I could not leave Nairobi fast enough, and when I finally did, I only had 15 days with her. She died from a heart attack at the Mediheal Hospital, Eldoret.

Life has not been the same since because my anchor is gone. Regaining my balance was not easy, but I feel seven times stronger, inspired by mum's life and knowing that I have to maintain her legacy.

Following mum's death, I embarked on social impact projects alongside the business. La Covi Campaign is a COVID-19 social media response project I started to create global awareness and sensitise communities using animations.

Later in 2020, I relocated to South Asia. Like in Spain, everything, including racism, is different, but I am learning to cope. It is creepy but amusing how people want to touch my hair while others avoid sitting next to me on the bus.

In everything, self-discipline is crucial, and understanding your purpose in life is the reason that makes me wake up each morning. I now know how to view life with different lenses and live by the Serenity Prayer – to change what I can and accept what I cannot – as my life journey continues. I choose to soldier on!

About The Author

Ivy Karushi Akii is a young African social entrepreneur passionate about transforming the lives of young women. She collaborates with like-minded organisations as an advisor, facilitator, speaker, and mentor to inspire young people to be leaders in the entrepreneurial space.

Ivy is the co-founder of I'm Baobab company that supports eco-friendly innovations in Kenya and Sae Company in South Korea which is focussed on providing inclusive and sustainable societal solutions using digital platforms. She is a co-founder of Beleven Company in Spain and the USA where she served as the company's 2nd CEO and 1st female CEO.

She is a co-creator of various community impact projects focusing on: utilising waste fabric to create aesthetic value on notebooks; sustainable fashion; COVID-19 advocacy; teenage pregnancy awareness, and recycling plastics to the fabric-circular economy.

Ivy is also an accomplished young leader in the World Organisation of Scout Movement.

Ivy can be contacted at:

Email: *ivyaki6@gmail.com*

LinkedIn: *https://www.linkedin.com/in/ivy-akii-socialentrepreneur/*

Facebook: *http://www.facebook.com/akikarushiivy.ivy*

STORY TWENTY TWO

Unique Path to Happiness

Everything we go through in life, leads us somewhere.

I sat in the bathroom staring at the white stick in my hand. Three minutes seemed like a lifetime. I waited, alternately looking at my watch, a crack in the floor tile and the stick. I had lost count of how many times I had done this. But then something happened that had never happened before. The two lines began turning blue! Not just one line, but both the lines! I couldn't believe my eyes which soon started to blur with the tears. I quickly ran and grabbed my camera. I took a picture before the lines faded.

Anyone who has taken a home pregnancy test, knows exactly what I'm talking about. Yes! I was finally pregnant. After all those years of trying, I had lived to see the day.

My husband and I had been married for 11 years. In the eyes (and mind) of the world, we should have had a child or two by now. Everyone around us was interested in when we were going to have babies. And I'm not talking just about our extended family and friends. Everyone was giving their two cents on how we could get pregnant.

For the first seven to eight years of our married life, we were busy building our careers, acquiring assets, travelling the world, finally living it out. But at 32, I knew I wasn't getting any younger. My husband felt settled in his job. Now was the time for us to start preparing for our family.

So, we started trying, keeping things casual at first. Eight months down the road, when just "trying" did not work, I began reading books and articles on the internet on "How to get Pregnant".

Months passed. With no success in sight, the big guns aka the ovulation test kit came out, with the intention to get the exact date for conception to take place. No more romantic dinners, just getting straight to business. Even sneaking out of work to come home during lunchtime.

When nothing seemed to work, we finally booked an appointment to see a specialist. He recommended some tests and checks. The results came in fine. He suggested if we don't fall pregnant naturally in the next few months, we could try other interventions.

But within a month of the visit, it looked like God had finally answered our prayers. I was going to be a MOM. I couldn't contain my excitement. But I didn't want to call my husband on the phone to share the news we had been waiting so desperately for. It was only four o'clock. So I had to wait.

Finally, when my husband got home that evening. I showed him the picture of the stick. Needless to say, he was the happiest man on earth. We contemplated telling the family but decided to hold off until the first trimester was over. Superstitious or cautious, or both perhaps.

We visited our doctor later that week. He suggested a blood test to confirm the pregnancy and a follow up appointment was given. Two days later we were back at the doctor's office beaming with joy. The doctor confirmed the pregnancy but said my hormone levels were lower than what's expected. He prescribed an oral medication and recommended I do a blood test every week to check the progress. This wasn't the news we were expecting but we took it as a small road block.

For the next few weeks, I went in for blood tests. There was some improvement in the hormone levels but not to what my doctor had hoped for. We continued with the medication and blood tests.

At 10 weeks, I was due for an ultrasound. As the doctor applied the cold gel on my belly, I was nervous and excited. Lying down in the freezing room, staring at the monitor, all I could remember was, this is the moment I had always dreamt of.

But it remained a dream. There was no fetal heartbeat. He pronounced the pregnancy "non-viable". I felt my own heart stop beating that moment.

After all these years, when I finally fell pregnant. How could this be?

We were devastated.

The doctor asked me to get a DNC and send the sample for biopsy, just in case. Next thing I know, instead of being offered a tissue to wipe my tears, I was being shoved a waiver to sign for the operation.

I signed. Got ready for the procedure which was to be done under general anaesthesia. All went fine and I was home by nightfall.

We decided to give ourselves some time to heal. Mostly emotionally. And started to try again a few months later. And to my surprise I fell pregnant again. This time we didn't want to get too excited and jinx it. We booked an appointment with the doctor and got the tests done.

Disappointingly, the hormone levels were low again. We were back to medication and weekly blood tests. I don't know if I was just getting used to being pricked or the nurses gained more experience. It didn't hurt so much anymore. But what hurt was the scan in the ninth week.

Verdict: A "non-viable" pregnancy again.

This time we skipped the whole D&C procedure and let nature take its course. I'll spare you details of the miscarriage. I pray no woman has to ever go through it.

This was the start of the lowest point in my life. I felt I was cursed. I must have said, felt or done something really bad in this life or in a past life to deserve this. I hid in my bathroom for hours and wept every day.

But I wasn't going to give up. I decided to wage war against God.

I called my doctor and told him I was ready for the intervention. I'll do whatever it takes to put a baby in my belly.

From there the rounds of IVF drugs started. I wasn't just being pricked in the arm for a blood test twice a week. I was also administering shots in my tummy, that too, by myself. I hate needles. But I forged ahead. And when the side effects like bloating, mood swings, headaches, restlessness and more, kicked in, I said to myself "Bring it on. I am not letting God win this time."

By now I was so desperate, I would do whatever someone would tell me that would help with conception.

What awaited was failure after failure. Even with the highest dosage possible my hormones wouldn't go up. In fact they were lower than what I was able to produce naturally. The doctor called this "a one in a million" case. So I changed doctors, hoping someone new could perform a miracle. The score now was:

God – 8. Neera – 0.

Earlier when I said the lowest point of my life had started. This was worse! I had failed.

I felt shame, and guilt. I blamed myself.

Maybe I should have not travelled so much, eaten healthier, not gone out partying, taken supplements, done more yoga, not used a tampon. The list was endless.

I hated myself.

To make things worse, I had not shared what I was going through with anyone. To the outside world we were a high-flying power couple with no responsibilities holding us back.

People envied us. Little did they know how we envied them. No one saw the heartache and loathing. I had become good at hiding it. But inside I was hurting.

I felt incomplete, incompetent, useless. The one thing only a woman can do, is to bear children. But why couldn't I? Why was I dealt a bad hand? Why couldn't I give that joy to my loving husband who not once made me feel any less?

We had an IUI cycle in Sydney which was unsuccessful. After consoling me, the doctor turned towards my husband and asked him how he was doing. He broke down. That's when I realised no-one had ever asked him. The pain and the suffering wasn't mine alone. He was silently hurting too. Not because we couldn't have children but because he couldn't see me go through the pain and the embarrassment. For me, he stayed strong.

We finally decided to tell our family what we had been going through. I wish we had earlier. Whilst they felt sad for us from there on they were our rock or shall I say our mountain. For the fear of being judged, we underestimated the support family had to offer. In fact, it was our parents who asked us to halt all the external interventions and just let it be. They chose to have a healthy and happy daughter/daughter-in-law over grandchildren.

This meant a lot to me. I realised I was important. I began to heal.

On the internet, I also found some forums and support groups for women who had been unable to conceive. Many had it much worse than me. It was comforting to know I wasn't alone in this journey. Opening up felt comforting. It might sound strange, but with them, I felt I belonged. I didn't need to explain what I was going through. That I tried everything. They simply understood. More importantly, they helped me understand, none of this was my fault.

I wasn't less.

I knew now, I had to move on. Find a path to the happiness I had been searching for. No more spiralling, rather flying upwards and onwards.

I made my amends with God. My win was God's win. We were on the same side.

On one of my work trips, I was fortunate to meet a wonderful vibrant soul, who regularly helped rescue dogs and other animals. She suggested we adopt a dog. For that I had to first overcome my fear of dogs. I had no choice. My heart was filled with so much love, I needed to nurture.

And that's how JD aka Jack Daniels, a three-year-old golden retriever (my first born and favourite child) came into my life eight years ago. And just as I said to people, we aren't planning for a second one, a year after, came along Kit Kat, my toy poodle who was also a rescue.

A few months later, encouraged by another dear friend, I quit my corporate job and started out on my own. I had never thought I had in me to become an entrepreneur. But I took the plunge. Running an events company was demanding but also very satisfying. Watching it grow and flourish gave me a purpose. I was at peace.

My guiding soul once said to me, "Everything we go through in life, leads us somewhere."

A year later, when I least expected, it seemed the stars, the planets, the whole freaking galaxy had aligned. A chance meeting with a friend who had recently adopted a baby, led to another life changing moment.

Six months later, my dream finally became true. Looking at those tiny little fingers, holding her in my arms, caressing her mostly bald head, I understood why everything happened. There was a plan for me. I just needed to be open to possibilities.

Today I have a very busy household filled with laughter, barks, playtime, bruises, tears but mostly love and happiness. My daughter turns six this year and her brother turns three. Both adopted at birth.

Finally, I feel complete.

To my wonderful sisters reading this story I would like to say, in life we will all have struggles and challenges. We cannot hide or run away from them. So it is up to you to choose your own path to happiness. Be it love, freedom, growth, peace, family or anything else. And in your journey, you will come across some amazing souls who will knowingly or unknowingly, guide and inspire you.

So, don't be afraid or let anything hold you back. Seek what you want, and like me, you too will find what you have been waiting for.

About The Author

Neera Gupta is an Entrepreneur, Writer, Event Organiser, TV host, Emcee, Champion Networker, Marketing Guru, Women Empowerment Ambassador, Charity worker, Publisher........ the list goes on. But one thing that most people don't know about her is that she is also a dentist!

From organising top class events to writing and publishing bestselling books, hosting and producing TV shows, presenting at seminars/workshops, working with and leading teams, empowering women from around the world, to giving back to the society by working with those in need. Neera believes in pushing boundaries and seeing things in different ways. Those who know her, know that she is up for any challenge the world throws at her, and always comes out a winner!

She lives in Singapore with her husband of twenty years, two young children – Sahana & Sarang and two fur kids - JD and Kit Kat.

Neera can be contacted at:

Email: *neera@globalinfluencers.sg*

LinkedIn: *https://www.linkedin.com/in/drneeragupta/*

Website: *www.globalinfluencers.sg*

STORY TWENTY THREE

Your Story is Your Legacy

Everyone has a story. And, like a snowflake, every story is unique - even if are a twin! Sharing your Story can be the greatest gift, but writing your story will be your greatest legacy.

Never, ever in a bazillion years did I envision myself as a writer.

And you, dear reader, may say: "Well, big whoop di do!"

The French philosopher Descartes coined the well-known phrase: "I think, therefore I am." To that, I will say: "I write, therefore I am forever!"

Recently I have been in the proximity of some discussion concerning what a person's legacy may constitute.

I know that many people consider their children and grandchildren their greatest legacies. To that, I say: "Bah, Humbug! Sentimental claptrap!"

You see, a couple of years ago, I attended (if that is the right word) a self-guided literary tour of the Melbourne Cemetery, and I learned something profound.

Did you know that it is rare for your grave to be attended by anyone after two generations have passed? So, in other words, when you are buried with full pomp and ceremony, your children and possibly grandchildren may tend your grave, but anyone after that is doubtful. That is why when you go to an old cemetery like the Melbourne Cemetery, you will see grave after grave with broken headstones or cavernous holes that look like a scene from the zombie apocalypse. Their descendants just don't care. Some legacy!

There are those amongst us mere mortals upon this earth who have the dollars and cents to leave a legacy by way of a building named in their honour or a hospital wing or some other "thing" that may last a few generations before it finally collapses or implodes or just disappears into dust.

However, if you write, there is a good chance of being read sometime in the future.

I refer to my friend René Descartes. His *Discourse on Method*, from which that famous quote "I think, therefore I am" is taken, was written in 1637.

And if you ever had the misfortune to attend an English-speaking high school of any kind, you will have been tortured for at least three years, equalling three plays by Shakespeare, who wrote in the late 1500s to early 1600s.

It gets better than that. We still refer to the works of Aristotle, the Ancient Greek Philosopher. His writings date to the 300s. Pliny the Elder, another Ancient Greek, wrote in the first century AD. And what about the hieroglyphics of the Ancient Egyptian tombs? It's all writing!!

So, I am sure you are starting to see my point.

Even in our modern age, we all know that anything you put on the interweb will be there forever. So, as I said earlier: I write, therefore I am forever.

To be serious now.....

Not everyone has children nor the money to create grand edifices in their names, but most educated people know how to write. (And in our modern age, you don't even have to be educated to write!)

I am one of the childless, penniless, however literate masses, and my legacy is that I can write. Worse still, is that I actually enjoy writing!

To date, I am the co-author of two Amazon bestselling self-help books, with more in the pipeline. However, I don't consider them my greatest works (yet).

My most outstanding literary achievement to date is far more humble.

Think back to the year 2020 and the COVID-19 pandemic that touched every corner of the globe.

Like many others, my workplace retreated to working from various desks, dining tables, and laptops balanced on quivering knees in workers' own homes.

Yippee-i-o-ki-ay (or any other shout of extreme happiness)! All my Christmases have come at once.

No more spending three hours per day commuting to and from work.

I get to see my cats all day. I get to do all my work at my pace etc., etc.

Yes, like most people, I know I worked harder than I ever did in the office, but at least I was at home.

However, that was okay for the first few weeks until I noticed that our team of about fifty people was starting to lose that connection we had when we saw each other every day.

Yes, we had the communal chat rooms set up, and we could have video meetings any time, but it just wasn't enough.

And then, as a writer, I had my brainiac idea!

I'll write an email every workday to our team just to keep us all connected. My boss and our Director were happy for me to do this, so off I went.

I wrote my first email in early April 2020 and my last one on the day I officially "retired" on 1 February 2021. In total, I wrote 207 emails/blogs to my colleagues, one on every working day from the day I started.

Now, these weren't two lines of "ra ra, go get 'em" pep talk every day. I wrote between 400 - 500 words about something. Some days I wrote about work-related issues, but mostly I wrote about "stuff."

I wrote about life in lockdown. I wrote about my garden and the things I saw for the first or for the first time in a long time as the year evolved. I sometimes wrote a photo essay, including a photo of a spectacular flower I found in my garden that was a tiny weed in reality.

I also wrote about the first shopping trip I went on with my friend/neighbour after our longest period of lockdown. I had a countdown for that trip, and there was great excitement and joy in going to Kmart of all places.

I wrote about things I heard or saw on the news. I wrote about anything I thought may be of interest or may amuse my colleagues.

I will admit that some days it was a struggle, and I had no idea what to write about, but I had made a commitment, and even though I wasn't sure at times that anyone was reading my emails, I had to write that email just in case someone was waiting on it.

However, there came a day when my Director acknowledged my efforts publicly in a staff meeting, adding that my efforts were making him look good with the higher-ups and that he was grateful for that. My colleagues then started to tell me that receiving my email was the highlight of their day.

No-one ever knew what I was going to write about, and for the staff who read the emails, it was a chance to be distracted from our sometimes challenging work. One colleague told me that he waited for my email every day so he could stop and have a coffee while he read it!

So now I am on a roll, and I write regularly. I believe that everyone has a story and that their story is their legacy. The story I have told above is just one of the many stories I have. As a writer, I collect stories like a child collects swap cards.

I am constantly reminded of the 1989 Guinness advertisement where the character says, "I like to watch." The ad is only 16 seconds long, but it always makes me laugh because I, too, like to watch. How else do I collect my stories about people and the things I see and hear?

Now many of you will be thinking, "She wrote some emails. Big deal."

They are a big deal because, you see, on the 13 March 2013, I suffered a stroke while driving home from an appointment.

That afternoon, I drove for 15 minutes in peak hour traffic to a suburb I had never gone to before, into a street I had never been in before. I did not injure or kill anyone, and I sustained no injuries.

I remember the ambulance paramedic telling me that they were going to put me in the ambulance, and therefore they wanted me to try and get out of the car. I can recall getting into the ambulance, and then the next thing I remember is waking to the throbbing noise and enclosed space of an MRI machine.

The human brain is an incredible organ, and it wants to protect you as much as it possibly can. There was no pain other than warning headaches, and I had no significant recollection of having a stroke. It did not hurt in any way.

To give you the *Readers Digest* abridged version – during recovery following a stroke, your brain is trying to reconnect all the neural pathways that break when your brain suffers the internal milkshake that is the experience of a stroke. Things you have seen, learned or done, even the most minor of past experiences, are viewed by your brain as brand new.

Re-establishing neural pathways, even if you have done something a million times before, is exhausting. You are in constant sensory overload. You sleep a lot – deep, deep, satisfying, and refreshing sleep. Gradually you can do more and more of what you used to do with confidence and without second-guessing. In most cases, the recovery you make in the first five years is as good as things will get.

I have no physical damage. Yet, my life has changed in ways that no-one else can see:

- I have developed seizures that are classified as epileptic but are atypical. They follow a set pattern, and I am always present through them. I could be talking to you and having one. You would never know unless I tell you that it is happening. There is nothing to see.
- I cannot smell or taste everything, and even the things I can taste, their taste varies in intensities from one time to another.
- I used to love reading, but now, it is a real chore. It is like a switch has been flipped somewhere in my brain.

- My formerly photographic memory is more like a lace curtain now. I remember bits and pieces but not everything.
- One of the worst things is that I forget the names of people, even those people who are closest to me. I also forget words randomly. You know that saying – "It's on the tip of my tongue?" I get that a lot.
- The other residual effect is that my brain now struggles to distinguish between noise and valuable information. I struggle to understand conversations at parties or any situation where there is a lot of ambient noise.

That is my real story. That is my legacy to share with the world. The more I share my story, whether it is on a stage or by writing about it, the greater my legacy is.

Now more than ever, when life is challenging on so many levels for so many people, it is time for everyone to share their stories.

If you don't know how to do that, find someone who can help. You don't have to be a writer to write your story. You don't have to be famous to have an exciting or worthy story. The simplest and most mundane stories can raise the spirits of and inspire a reader.

Technology and the gift of co-authored anthologies can allow everyone to be an author and proclaim, "I write, therefore I am forever!"

Your story is your legacy. Start writing now!

About The Author

Anna Von Zinner is a positively determined human being. She is an author, thought leader, international speaker and unafraid.

Having a stroke at 50, she found a new purpose and direction in life. She has chosen to live life to its full capacity and shares her stories, discoveries and plans with others travelling a similar road.

Having a stroke does not have to be a death sentence, but the choices you make afterwards can be. She chooses to be unafraid.

Anna can be contacted at:

Website: *www.annavonzinner.com*

LinkedIn: *www.linkedin.com/in/Anna-Von-Zinner-070/*

Facebook: *www.facebook.com/anna.vz.54*

Raising Your Voice

We all have an opinion, a view or simply, thoughts about things that happen to or around us. Some think, some speak, but the majority do nothing.

But what if you are the one who does something and takes charge of a situation, turning challenges into inspiration. Don't you want to be heard and even help those who don't dare to speak? Well, we want to hear from you!

At **GLOBAL INFLUENCERS PUBLISHING HOUSE**, we publish books that inspire, motivate, empower, teach, enrich, connect, inform, stimulate or simply make you laugh.

OUR OBJECTIVE is to connect the hearts and minds of our international readers and authors through the power of words. **THE TEAM** who works behind the scenes, around the clock, making all this magic happen, have been handpicked for their skill, talent, dedication and passion for achieving our objective. So, if you have a **STORY** to share, send us a message on: **contactus@globalinfluencers.sg**

You can also join the **#MY VOICE FORUM**, which provides a network for like-minded women worldwide to come together to talk about things that matter. This is a space where we can agree, disagree, or agree to disagree but without any judgement, discuss issues and challenges faced, lend a listening ear or a helping hand to one another, find solutions and ultimately take action to make change happen. To find out more, go to: **www.facebook.com/groups/myvoiceforum**

Together we will embark on a new journey to make life happen on our terms by creating the world we deserve to live in.

Coming Soon

#myvoice
Vol. 2
A Collective Memoir by Women of Substance

Global Influencers Publishing House

#myvoice GLOBAL INFLUENCERS PUBLISHING HOUSE